THE CLOWN
IN YOU

Caroline Dream

THE CLOWN IN YOU

a guide to contemporary clowning

General Editor: Alejandro Navarro
Editor: Richard Drain
Cover design: Alejandro Navarro

ISBN-13: 978-84-616-9652-9

For Alex and Amara

Contents

Acknowledgements

Without the support, encouragement and love of all these people I would have given up during the long process of writing this book. I am deeply grateful to them all.

Alex Navarro, without whom I would never have learnt so much, trusted myself so much or written so much. His unconditional support, his suggestions and comments, and his unswerving interest in everything I wrote have made this book a communal project rather than the work of one individual.

My daughter, Amara, who has filled my life with joy from the moment she was born.

My father, who throughout my childhood, kindled my enthusiasm for stories, books and theatre. Knowing I could always count on his unwavering support and encouragement for all my clowning projects (including this one) has meant more to me than words can express.

My mother, who through her passion for art and artists, taught me to love deeply, trust in my own expressivity, and seek happiness through living a creative life.

My sisters, with whom I learned the pleasures of laughter, rebellion and play.

Juan Carlos Valdovinos, whose enthusiasm, wisdom and generosity gave me the courage to keep writing in the early stages of the creative process.

Leonardo Garcia, an excellent clown and master psychologist, who was always willing to clarify my doubts and answer my questions.

My clown teachers, who opened my eyes, stripped me bare of all but my red nose, and encouraged me to go further than I ever thought possible.

My clown friends, those warm and bold individuals who love this art with the same eager excitement as I do, who have made me laugh with my whole being, who have expanded my heart and who, without hesitation, have willingly offered me their time and knowledge.

The professional clowns throughout the world who, through their passion, dedication and boundless creativity, have inspired me to continue clowning. Seeing them in action has nourished, informed and influenced my writing.

My students, without whom I would never have sought so many answers to the whys and wherefores of clowning technique. They have been my guides in class and also when writing. I am grateful for their generosity, courage and willingness to learn.

Author's note:

The teaching method, as set forth in this book, was developed between 1998 and 2011, in the courses I taught alongside Alex Navarro. All the experiences described herein are the result of our mutual collaboration and creativity. In certain chapters I have changed the names of the students to protect the trust they placed in me. Real names are quoted with both name and surname.

Preface

The Clown In You is a book written from the heart. It is a theoretical and practical tool, as useful to those who are starting out in the world of clowning as to those who are looking for reasons to do so.

Reading it will help you deepen your understanding of the technical requirements of clowning and the clown's philosophical mind space. Within its pages you'll also find a detailed analysis of the essential principles of clowning, ways to tackle or overcome the problems you are bound to encounter when learning to clown, examples of student improvisations, useful games and exercises, and some insightful quotes from professional clowns and international clown teachers. The book offers an overview of the pedagogical methodology we developed over a fifteen year period, with many references to the ways in which we helped our students through their resistances and on to breakthroughs in expressing their clowns.

Caroline and I first teamed up to run a series of clown courses in Las Vegas for Cirque du Soleil artists in 1998. We were both passionate about our art and saw the need to develop a methodology which would offer students the opportunity to continually grow in confidence and expertise. We therefore embarked on a long-term clowning adventure, teaching hundreds of courses for beginner, intermediate and advanced students as well as for professionals wanting to create new routines. Our work took us to many countries around the world; Spain, Portugal, Italy, Germany, Peru Puerto Rico, Columbia, Costa Rica and Mexico. In 2010 Caroline continued developing our pedagogy through solo courses of varying lengths and levels. Her students have long since recognised her ability to "x-ray" their personalities and expose their clown with surprising ease. With all her many years of experience, experimentation and investigation she is, without a doubt, an expert voice in the field.

Clown training, as we know it today, is a recent phenomenon. During the last century, in the circus, the knowledge of this craft was handed down from father to son, or between circus families. Acrobats, trapeze artists or jugglers would turn to clowning when they were unable to continue within their own discipline. Having lived with clowns and watched them throughout their entire lives, these artists had imbibed the routines, the timing and the presence of the professionals and were thus able to do justice to the acts they inherited. Today, all that has changed. Students now have opportunities to train with clown masters from many different countries, to see (either live or virtually) great clowns in action, and to experiment with both traditional and self-created material.

Perhaps for this reason, in the last decade, many more people have become interested in discovering their clown. The curious, the courageous, and the intrepid choose to participate in a clown course because they are no longer content to just slump on their sofas. They rightly suspect that the red nose may open the door on a world that was always there but that, with the passage of the years, was somehow forgotten.

The search and rescue process of the clown varies considerably. How easy it proves to be depends on one's personality, life experiences and personal life circumstances. Some people have an innate talent; they'll walk on stage and already possess a natural connection with the audience, excellent comic timing, great ideas and a wicked sense of humour. Others will have to work on these things over an extended period of time.

The question of whether everyone can be a clown has two answers. If you are thinking in purely professional terms, the answer is no. But the fact is that most people who enroll in a clown course these days have no professional ambitions, in the same way that not everyone who studies guitar wants to perform for an audience. Many people undertake this journey of discovery for personal reasons; to live an unusual experience, overcome certain fears, improve their sense of humour, or simply to let their hair down and learn to enjoy life more. In this context therefore, the answer would be a resounding yes. Everyone can clown.

At this point, I should clarify that one does not become a clown by simply donning a red nose. In fact, there are many professionals today who do not use one on stage. We have found, however, that wearing a red nose greatly helps the novice to shake off their normality. But there is much more to this art than the externals. Clowns need bucket loads of creativity, the ability to create rapport with their audience, a willingness to share their particular vision of the world and a capacity for honesty that far exceeds the norm.

Many times I have come across people who have asked me what I do, and when I responded, "I'm a clown" they've insisted, "yes, but... how do you earn a living?", as if they thought it impossible to make a living working as a clown. It is still difficult for many people to understand that being a clown, as Annie Fratellini once said, "is a spiritual state, but also a trade". This is, unfortunately, not the only confusion we have to deal with around our profession.

A few years ago I accompanied Caroline to a performance she was giving, and while she set up her props and got ready, I went for a drink at the theatre bar. I'd only just begun sipping my coffee when the old man sitting next to me asked, "Have you any idea what's on tonight?"

"My wife's performing, she's a clown," I replied.

"Come on!" he said, "don't say that about your wife!" He seemed shocked and annoyed.

"Why?" I asked him, "did I say something I shouldn't have?"

"You should call her an actress, not a clown," he said accusingly, as if by my choice of words I was intentionally trying to demean her.

I tried to make him understand that being a clown is as worthy of respect as being a mechanic, a doctor, or anything else, but he remained doubtful. This is but one example of the mistaken beliefs that so many people have about clowns. Little do they know what it really means to be a clown!

Imagine for a moment a world inhabited exclusively by clowns. Wars would be fought with cream pies, failures would be applauded, the economy would be turned on it's head, two plus two would equal five, and a present would consist of a cardboard box and a stick, which would immediately become a pirate ship and a spyglass. The world would be a place where innocence and tenderness would be the order of the day, where making eye contact, showing vulnerability or sharing feelings would be an everyday occurrence. Playing would be obligatory, laughter would always be present and the greatest responsibilities in life would be happiness and fun.

Alex Navarro

1
Introduction

Information on clowning technique has, for far too long, remained a professional secret. It's only very recently that clowns have begun to write about their art and share their knowledge as teachers, but even so much remains to be categorized and clarified. Clowns have been misrepresented and misunderstood for decades. They've been stereotyped and reduced, considered unimportant by the vast majority of modern day society. Clowns? They're a bunch of idiots!

This book rejects outright this concept of clowns. It is instead a vindication of all the talent, skill and audacity needed to encounter, encourage and set free the clown in you. Making people laugh is much more fascinatingly complex than you can at first imagine. Clown students don't just have to learn the basics of being funny, there is much, much more to it than that. Thus I am proposing a radical shift in the general perception of this ancient and heart-warming art. It is my intention with this book to convince all who read it that contemporary clowns are in fact a bunch of *exceptional* beings.

Clowning, like all the other arts, requires you to be a creative channel of expression. What you express as a clown is your essence, your life experience and your personal vision of the universe. That's why there are no age limits, no previous study requirements, no particular comic personality required to start on the clown trail. You really only have to be prepared to share yourself, with humility and humanity, and accept that this particular journey has no foreseeable end.

From the start and throughout your clown training, you'll find that there are actually two major pathways to follow; the outer (what happens on stage) and the inner (what happens inside you). Having written this book back to front, the last chapter first, the introduction last (I am a clown myself after all), my conclusion is that there are deep parallel discoveries to be made. These discoveries are first centred on your desire to perform and make people laugh; but they go hand in hand with more significant discoveries about who you are, how your thoughts are influencing your actions and reactions, and how cultivating humour can transform your reality and give you the liberating experience of freedom: a freedom that is of the mind, body and soul.

Some professional clowns have chosen to focus almost exclusively on the outer path, but I personally have been unable to ignore the profound wisdom lying just beneath the surface of all clowning methodology. My students have only reinforced my belief that clowning is a healing art as well as a fun thing to do professionally. However, unlike the majority of healing techniques, its aim is not to cure the sick, but rather to uncover and celebrate people's inherent aliveness. This celebration of *being*, which permeates clown technique, is offset by a complete down to earth-ness. It's a compelling combination, and one that allows everyone, no matter what their personal beliefs or social status, to benefit from experiencing their clown. So I ask you to keep an entirely open mind. Be prepared to be surprised by things you don't know. I've had the pleasure of living the clown experience for over twenty-five years and yet I still feel there's so much more to explore.

2
About clowns

Are there different types of clowns?

The clown I've researched and written about in this book is contemporary, new generation, and unisex. Clowns, of course, have made appearances throughout history but it was not until the nineteenth century that they began using the red nose and creating routines for circus audiences. These clowns, the traditional or classic clowns, are still a source of inspiration for many contemporary clowns, but many others have reinvented their art, following instead their own tastes and ideas. Most have stopped wearing the traditional costumes and have abandoned the circus ring in order to keep experimenting, evolving and reaching new audiences. At least here in Spain, clowns can now be found performing in hospitals, businesses, trains, streets, theatres, libraries, shops, schools, restaurants, zoos — in fact just about anywhere. This recent "revolution" in clowning is in fact the result of individual and collective experimentation, of clowns embracing other techniques, cultures and artistic disciplines.

Contemporary new generation clowns are only just beginning to attempt to classify themselves, but there's still a lot of resistance within the profession to labelling per se. So it's hardly surprising that there is so much confusion about clowns. Grouping ourselves under this one generic umbrella is creating problems, even for ourselves. I often go to see clowns performing but I hardly ever know what I will encounter. It's not just a question of quality or talent, it's also a question of style and taste. Sometimes, watching clowns perform, I feel like a jazz lover at a barn dance, I can appreciate the enthusiasm but little else.

I personally think we'd do ourselves, and our public, a favor in clarifying our differences and also what unites us. I know this is a difficult task because clowning is an art in constant evolution but now that there is so much more interest in clowning, and so many more students wanting to learn, our art must begin to define itself so that it can keep growing, improving and reaching out to more and more people.

What is a clown?

When I started interviewing professional clowns I, like almost every interviewer before me (and probably all to come too), always asked this standard yet terrible question: What is a clown?

After the first batch of interviews I realised my mistake. This is actually the one question all clowns would rather not be asked. My own feeling when confronted with this question is always resignation. Why? Because it's impossible to answer correctly without writing a book (which is why at last I've written one). A short answer has got to be poetic, giving the illusion of having answered but leaving a lot to interpretation. How can you describe a state of comic being in a couple of sentences? It's a bit like trying to explain the experience of true love to someone who's never been in love. You use words to describe your craft, but you're conscious of the fact that your experience of it is, by nature, subjective. An honest answer to the question would therefore be: "Don't ask me that, please! Ask me what a clown is not."

Now that's a much easier question to answer. We would all answer similarly. "A clown is not a fancy dress costume you put on or a character you build from the outside and perform. A clown is definitely not a red nose or a stereotype."

But as you'll invariably be asked at some point in your training, What is a clown? maybe you'd like a short answer to pull out of your sleeve. Here are some of the poetic answers I received from the professionals before I stopped asking, I hope they help!

> "Clowns can use or not use a tiny mask but they nevertheless allow themselves to be seen completely naked. Possessing this immense freedom, clowns make people laugh by showing themselves as they are. They are communicators, capable of moving, provoking and infuriating."
>
> *Lila Monti, Argentina*

> "A clown is a little bit of anarchy and a lot of transgression."
>
> *Jason El Guapo (Pata de Perro), Mexico*

> "Clowns make us laugh and dream at the same time. They make us laugh and cry from the heart, the gut and the soul."
>
> *Hilary Chaplain, U.S.A.*

> "A clown is you yourself but characterized — a caricature of the individual where we still see the original person, but certain aspects are highlighted, exaggerated, or appear eccentric."
>
> *Andrés Aguilar, Mexico*

"After twenty-three years working on the question I feel that the clown is a place. At first it seemed like a place where one looked for laughter, but now I feel it's a place where one allows oneself to be, without fear, without trying to prove anything to anyone. And from this place one is then able to mobilize those that are watching."

Wendy Ramos, Peru

"I think there's a magic chamber inside the individual and that the clown is a guide to reaching it. Through the physical, a clown can assist in tapping the memories and the knowledge that's inside the human condition. It is the process of becoming human."

Ira Seidenstein, Australia

"What I know for certain about my clown is that she is the most precious thing I have. She is my difference, my way of understanding the world. I am working with the following things: who I am, what I am passionate about, what I want to explain, and what I want to give to others."

Pepa Plana, Spain

Has everyone got a clown inside them?

This is another frequent question, but much easier to answer. Yes. Everyone has a clown identity, a *clown-id* (Freud was too serious and hard working to notice it). Everyone can, with a little help, experience the clown self that abides within them, the self that just *is*; fun loving, fun and funny. In fact, the moment you put your organised, realistic, critical and moralizing self aside you will find him/her with ease.

S/he is waiting in the wings of your consciousness, some-what impatiently, ready to grab the first opportunity you give him/her to be centre stage.

The problem is that until you've actually experienced your clown, even for the briefest moment, this will be hard to believe. Hard to believe too how *addictive* letting this crazy version of yourself run loose can be. Clowns breathe life and lightness into people. My students are usually amazed and delighted after an encounter with their more vibrant and reckless self.

There's a generalized idea that this clown identity is act-ually the inner child — but it's not. Clowns are not children, though they have obviously not lost sight of childhood nor ceased to observe children. Clowns have incorporated aspects of both but they are not frozen in time, they're quite capable of very adult attitudes, ideas and actions. Sex and sexuality, for instance, are some clowns' favourite topics.

Each clown is unique and grows over time. If you asked any professional, "What is your clown like?" they'd all tell you something completely personal. Clowns call themselves clowns because they recognise the art that is their playground but the individuals that are playing there each have their own charisma. If you have already experienced your clown you'll know that it's a lot like tuning yourself in to a specific frequency. When you're receiving the signal you still feel like you, just with fewer complexes and more creativity.

How do I tune in to the clown frequency?

Because each individual, and their clown, are unique, every-one needs to find their own particular way of "plugging in". Clown teachers can point students in the right direction but whether they open the door and let their clown out is up to them. Like many teachers I use games and clown exercises as a means of stimulating awareness, openness and trust as well as teaching clown psychology, stage craft and, of course, clown technique.

I make students improvise rather than prepare routines because it's a far more valuable learning tool, even for experienced clowns. I do sometimes ask intermediate or advanced students to prepare material, but I always warn them that they may not get to perform all that they've prepared. More often than not they lose their clowns as soon as they plan their actions, and also lose contact with the audience; together this means they are learning nothing useful.

If students are forced to improvise, extraordinary and funny things happen. Sometimes, the material that emerges can be a whole lot funnier than many professional performances. There is a useful definition of improvisation in Wikipedia which describes it as "the practice of acting, singing, talking and reacting, of making and creating, in the moment and in response to the stimulus of one's immediate environment and inner feelings. This can result in the invention of new thought patterns, new practices, new structures or symbols, and/or new ways to act. This invention cycle occurs most effectively when the practitioner has a thorough intuitive and technical understanding of the necessary skills and concerns within the improvised domain."

Clowning and improvisation go hand in hand. Clowns are by nature spontaneous, impulsive and inventive. People, however, do not always feel very inventive, nor are they able to let themselves be clowns at the drop of a hat. Learning to tune in to your clown whenever you want and under any circumstances takes time and dedication. Assimilating clown technique will give you valuable resources and the confidence to use them in your improvisations. You'll also start acquiring physical or emotional information about your clown that will make finding him/her that much easier. As with any skill, it's a matter of practice makes perfect. If you practise being fully alive and letting yourself *be*, if you practise noticing other people and making them laugh, wherever you are, whoever you're with, you'll soon discover the exact frequency of your clown.

Are there differences in teaching techniques?

Previous clown generations were actually quite reticent when it came to sharing their clowning knowledge with newcomers. Clowning technique was passed down through the generations of circus families but rarely to those who came from "the outside". Bearing in mind that clowns freely copied each others' gags and routines without paying royalties, it's understandable that what couldn't be stolen, their experience, they kept to themselves. Four decades ago a handful of valiant pioneers began to teach clown in Europe (Jacques Lecoq, Philippe Gaulier, Pierre Byland, and Annie Fratellini), but in recent years the number of clown teachers offering courses has multiplied considerably. Even so, clown academies are still few and far between.

If you've already started your training and have begun to observe and analyse clown shows, you'll have also discovered that surprisingly, every clown teacher and every professional clown seems to have a different piece of the immense and complicated jigsaw puzzle that makes up the art of clowning. Some teachers will undoubtedly contradict or disagree with others. This is unavoidable. There is no absolute truth, just a personal one, and it's actually up to you to find your own, not adopt someone else's.

Clown teachers are guides who can help you find your clown and understand how to develop and nurture him/her.

They can play an important role in helping you progress, both on the inner and outer path. Unfortunately there are still teachers who use physical or psychological abuse as part of their training method, believing that this profession is not for the weak spirited. That may be so, but having taught clowning for over a decade, I have come to believe that such abuse, albeit used as a means of releasing the clown in students, for many acts merely as a deterrent and for some can create lasting damage. In an education process that is in itself demanding, elusive and psychologically challenging, the teaching aids that are indispensable are encouragement, generosity and compassion.

At the beginning of my teaching career I made the mistake of making impossible demands on students, pushing them too hard and too fast, but I soon became aware that it didn't actually improve their ability to perform better. Also, I discovered that just about everyone beats themselves up in clown classes, using their own personal mental baseball bat. If anything, students need to be made aware that hitting themselves over the head with their own negative criticism is the very worst thing they can do to. Clowns shrink and disappear when people become afraid, or feel unsafe or belittled. Also, such criticism is often misguided, springing from the ridiculous idea that clowning can be learnt instantly. Clowning is like any other art in that it can take years to perfect. Therefore the only bat I let them use to vent their frustration is an inflatable one.

Is aggressive humour really funny?

Perhaps because the aggressive formula in clown training has not been questioned and eradicated in many clown classrooms, aggressive humour has sometimes spilled out on stage. I am well aware that what people find funny can vary enormously, but aggressive humour, which means the use of humour to degrade and manipulate others, is actually not at all compatible with clown philosophy. Anyone who has really delved into their art would know that clowns do not seek to dominate anyone. On the contrary, they are motivated freedom seekers.

Aggressive "clowns" do have their followers, I must admit. Cruelty breaks all taboos and is therefore appealing to some people. Audiences sit gripped by pleasure and fear, pleasure at watching someone else being humiliated, fear of being the next victim. They may not be aware of it, but their enjoyment denotes an underlying conviction that the person being humiliated actually deserves to be mistreated; that muscular men are derisory, that men without muscles are ridiculous too, that fat women are deformed, that thin women are sex objects, that all children are brats, etc.

Playing on stereotypes is an easy way to get a laugh but reveals very poor levels of creativity, sensitivity and affectivity. It's tempting, when in a position of power, to make fun of the vulnerable; but it's not very positive in purpose. It's a disguised form of violence — and violence only creates more violence. It is a dangerous game to play, for sooner or later someone is bound to turn on you. In fact you run the risk of having all the audience turn against you because abuse activates strong emotions in people; indignation, fear, anger, insecurity, sadness, etc. Suffering of this kind is hard to ignore for long, the audience will see your victims suffer and begin to feel uneasy. They'll become conscious of the fact that shaking that child like a sack of potatoes is not funny at all, or that the man you just jumped on is actually hurt, or that the woman who just refused to get down on her knees has the right to say "no".

Being on stage is a privilege the audience bestows on you because you have proclaimed yourself an artist. What art you wish to demonstrate is up to you but I feel that a positive rather than negative use of power and humour is integral to the art of clowning. Clowns first expose their own ridiculousness, only then do they gain the authority to laugh at others' absurdities.

What's the alternative?

A clown friend of mine told me that humour is the language clowns use to share their stories, emotions and adventures. I asked him to write something about that for this book and he agreed. A week later he sent me the following;

> *"I've been writing for over an hour about "humour" and my evolution is:*
>
> *When I've written three paragraphs I re-read what I've written, I don't like it, I re-write what I've written, I read, I don't like it, I correct it again, I read, I think I'm not explaining it very well, I re-write, I re-read, this is not what I want to say, I re-write, re-read, I'm sure no one'll understand it, I read, crying I re-write, I feel sorry for myself, I write, I'm useless, I re-write, I scratch my head, I re-read, re-write, re-cry, re-scratch, re-don't like what I've written, re-correct everythinggggggggg... ..*
>
> *Conclusion: I DON'T KNOW HOW TO WRITE ABOUT HUMOUR."*

This friend of mine, Carlo Mô, is a highly successful professional clown. He's a constant stream of hilarity on and off stage, how come he doesn't know how to explain humour?

Odd as it may seem from the outside, humour per se is not a subject taught in clown classes. We don't teach people to have a sense of humour, we assume everyone has one and that it just needs a little encouragement, if that. What we do teach is how to make people laugh, which obviously involves learning how to be funny, but the process isn't intellectual. There are no fixed funny formulas because *how* and *when* a particular gag is performed is almost more important than the gag in itself.

Learning how to make people laugh is very complex. There are multiple layers of information and skill to assimilate and practise. All these involve humour but each tackles a different aspect of it. Your clown will use your personal sense of humour at every opportunity, but s/he will also adopt a more universal style of humour when s/he deems it convenient. Positive humour is universally appreciated, being a humour style that promotes psychological health and well being. Adopting this style makes a clown's job easier because the laughter it creates is cathartic, and that means audiences will become more and more willing to laugh. Positive humour involves maintaining a positive outlook on life even in the face of adversity, being able to laugh at one's own humanity without losing one's self-esteem, and facilitating good relationships between people by dispersing emotional tensions.

Humour is in greater and greater demand in modern day society. After decades under the dominance of seriousness, the competitive work ethic and material accumulation, people have finally understood that true happiness lies elsewhere. They now yearn for lasting joy and the release that laughter gives them. Clowns offer an alternative choice. Their art encourages people to play, be themselves, find their inner joy, take greater risks, follow their instincts and open their hearts.

3
The good clown's handybook

I know that most people associate clowns with the red nose — so much so in fact that they think that just by wearing one you become a clown, instantly. But there's a huge difference between wearing a red nose and *acting like* a clown and actually *being* one. If someone uses a clown costume and just imitates the stereotyped version of a clown, they're not actually *being* a clown at all, they're hiding behind a cliché. The personal risk they're taking is practically nil. But if someone is *being* a clown they're putting themselves on the line, risking ridicule through displaying their own absurdity and giving free rein to their personal brand of craziness.

It's actually very easy to spot the difference. If you're watching clowns perform and don't feel that they're communicating something honest, vibrant or real it means they are actually just representing clown characters, as actors would. Their performance will feel superficial, without heart or soul, because their physical and vocal expressions are filtered and distorted, not altogether natural. On the other hand, if you sense that the clowns you're watching are inviting you into their personal universe, reacting to what occurs there within their own emotional and creative framework, making you laugh with them and love them, then you can be sure that you're watching authentic clowns in action.

The clown stereotype

The clown in its stereotyped form appeared in the 1970's when mime artists began wearing costumes and make-up that was similar if not identical to the circus clowns of the time. Some of these artists even wrote books about how to be clowns but, because they were mimes and not clowns, the books they wrote were manuals on how to imitate clowns, not be authentic clowns. For one reason or another the authentic clowns didn't clarify, at least in writing, the enormous differences between their art and the mime's art. Therefore these "clowning" manuals, and the mime-clown, heavily influenced future generations of clown students and performers who, through lack of alternative information, turned to them and took them at face value. They unknowingly started mimicking the mimes, hundreds of clown imitators started popping up everywhere and before anyone realised it, the idea of clowns as red-nosed face-pullers with exaggerated gestures became deeply rooted in the collective unconscious.

I've spent more than twenty-five years looking for information about the true art of clowning; through courses, conversations and my own experiments. At the beginning, having hardly studied clown in any depth, I created a clown show for children in the purest "mime clown character" style. For two years I performed regularly in schools around my home town. Before every show I'd practise my emotional expressions in a mirror, attempting to improve and perfect them but instead making them mask-like, completely unfelt and automatic. I thought this was the way to become a good clown, with perfectly honed facial expressions of stupidity, but in reality I was getting further and further away from being a clown at all. Fortunately, I was not unaware that something was amiss: I could feel the tension and fear every time I went out to perform, I didn't really connect to the audience and, worse still, my show wasn't very funny.

So I decided to go and study at a circus school and chose Fooltime in Bristol (which now no longer exists). At the time, it was the only school in Britain offering year long programmes in circus skills and the clown teachers there were Franki Anderson and John Lee. It was fantastic having these two professionals open up my eyes to the true art of clowning. Franki gave us classes twice a week; she called me "the sergeant" because of my physical rigidity and the military uniform I metaphorically put on every time I performed. She encouraged me with tenderness to relax and not try so hard, but it wasn't easy for me. I'd spent too long nurturing my bad habit and without my fixed, mask-like expressions I felt too exposed. But, by the year's end, I knew I had to get rid of them all, come what may, in order to find my true clown and enjoy her fully.

My apprenticeship lasted years, in fact as many years as I've been clowning. I'd say it's difficult for any clown to consider themselves "master" of their art. Personally, I feel there's always something new to learn, especially because, as I grow and change, so does my clown. If you clown for years you'll discover the same thing. Clowns are not static characters, nor can they attain a state of eternal perfection, but that's what makes them interesting. My clown keeps surprising me and now that I'm capable of letting her do this, it feels great to perform. So, having experienced both how not to be and how to be an authentic clown I can honestly say that the latter is much more satisfying, both for oneself and everyone else too.

Automatic actions and reactions

On the clown initiation courses, I don't immediately hand out red noses. First, I ask my students to play and just be themselves on stage. Even so, something strange happens to some people the moment they put on a red nose. Suddenly they lose all their naturalness. They come out on stage with forced happiness, use a silly voice, pretend to trip up, simulate falling, act like two year olds, etc. They take great pains in doing senseless things and then ask for a round of applause or some other forced response from their audience, even though they actually haven't done anything applaudable at all. Obviously no-one laughs, in fact there's usually an incredulous silence and looks of irony or blankness from the other students sitting in the audience.

This has happened so frequently that Alex and I gave a name to the phenomenon: The Good Clown's Handybook. This handybook is full to brimming with convenient automatic actions and easy-to-use false reactions. The image of a manual is useful in that it treats the problem as a whole, and offers an easy solution: Throw the book in the bin!

Automatic action is motivated by a need to *do* something on stage. Students move, gesticulate or talk in excess but are not present in any of these actions. They don't feel what each action provokes, either in themselves or their audience, and nor do they take pauses, sometimes not even for breathing! When action is automatic the brain stops functioning, then comedy is just about impossible because doing for doing's sake takes over.

Comedy is reliant on things appearing real and full of life. Clowns need to be present and alive to achieve this and not on auto-pilot. Their actions and expressions are therefore specific and purposeful. Their movements are used to highlight something they find comical, to create a ridiculous effect, to set up a gag or to involve others in their game. In improvisations clowns achieve this through listening, feeling the moment, watching the audiences reaction, feeling what needs to be done and what they want to do.

> "If your clown partner kicks you on your rear end during an improvisation and you immediately get angry, it's usually because you've reacted automatically. If instead you allowed yourself just to feel, who knows... maybe you actually enjoyed it! That would be the start of a great clown game!"
> *Alex Navarro*

The most common **automatic reactions** are:
- Someone comes close and looks you in the eyes: you fall in love.
- Someone gets hurt: you console them.
- Someone openly rejects you: you get sad or cry.
- Someone smiles at you: you smile back and become happy.

These reactions (and many others) are often expressed in an exaggerated, pantomimed way but not always. The stereotyped gestures are the easiest to spot, for example sadness; hunched shoulders, drooping head, the corners of the mouth pulled down and fisted hands wiping imaginary tears away.

How can you tell if you are using The Good Clown's Handybook?

It's easy to find out. Wave at a friend right now, say "hello" (if there's no one about, imagine someone you like in front of you). Now, wave and say "hello" to someone you don't know. Take the time to do it now.

What happened? Did you notice any differences? Or did you just repeat the same wave, the same tone and the same quality of voice? Were there differences in your facial, gestural or vocal expressions? Did it feel natural both times? Did you *feel* different? (and by *feel* I don't just mean emotionally; your sensory perceptions and your basic instincts can also be *felt*). If you were really present both times then you can skip the rest of this chapter, if not, keep reading.

False behaviour

False behaviour when clowning is usually due to one of the following:

1. The stereotyped child

If you're still in the process of finding your clown, avoid any stereotypical behaviour like the plague, particularly infantile attitudes or gestures such as: pretending to be shy, twisting your clothing in your hands, using a childish squeak of a voice, becoming tense in the facial area, etc.

If any of this sort of behaviour crops up in a clown class I stop the person immediately. I'll then ask them directly, "How old are you?" This always produces a laugh from the other students because it's so obvious from the outside that they're far older than they're pretending to be. The person on stage doesn't find the question funny. They don't understand what I'm trying to get them to admit. Normally their resistance is such that they'll refuse to say their real age, offering up instead the one they've adopted (usually somewhere between five and ten years old). In this case I repeat the initial question until they tell me their true age, which can sometimes take awhile, even once they've understood that there's no escape. However, when they finally give up fighting the obvious and confess to being an adult, their whole expression changes. Suddenly they are there; honestly, openly, simply, there. And it's a joy to see.

Some people assimilate the experience instantly and never return to the stereotype but others find it incredibly difficult to lay aside this particular mask. I've found using humour always helps in these circumstances. My favourite tongue in cheek nudge is the following:

If I see a student returning to child-like behaviour I ask them to tell me their name. This is something so simple that they respond genuinely. If they say "Charlie", for instance, I'll then ask them, "Charles senior or Charlie junior?" Most times this is enough to get them smiling and returning to their true age but if they resist I'll add, "Charlie, could you go back stage and tell your older brother to come out here?" This allows "Charlie" to leave the stage with his dignity intact, laughing even, and also allows Charles senior his turn, returning with good humour and an invitation to be more creative. Charles senior can then beg forgiveness for the deplorable behaviour of his younger brother, or he can threaten his baby brother backstage, or argue with him about revealing everything to their parents, he can even have a full blooded fight with him if he wants to! Whatever way he chooses to deal with the situation will inevitably be received with cheers and laughter and this success will lodge in his mind, reinforcing the re-programming of his behavioural patterns on stage.

Why is it so important to avoid the child stereotype? For the simple reason that your clown is as old as you are. Maybe you are a child at heart but even in this case that child will be real, not a stereotype.

A real child expresses their emotions in surprising ways. My daughter got lost when she was four years old, a frightening situation if ever their was one, but when at last I found her she wasn't even crying. Her way of expressing the terrible fear she was feeling was through sucking fiercely on her shirt sleeve — it was completely soaked with saliva!

If you actually observe children's behaviour these days you'll see that they don't use any of the stereotyped gestures adults attribute to them. Modern day children, at least in Europe, seem to grow up faster and get with it far earlier than children did previously. By the time they're five years old, the vast majority are well versed in being the centre of attention, at six they've learnt about fashion and how to be cool, at eight they can convincingly imitate adult behaviour and by ten they actually think they are adults. Real children surprise us, constantly.

2. The social smile

Smiling at other people is of-course a good way of showing them that you are friendly, open and loving, but only if the smile you produce is real and not unnaturally prolonged. If others detect any falseness or hollowness in your smile they will actually distrust you or judge you negatively, not positively. The social smile, or automatic smile in social situations, is often a cover up for feelings you don't want others to see. That's why, for your clown, it's a straight jacket. If you always enter the stage smiling you've made the decision that, whatever occurs, whatever you find there, is alright by you... you'll be pleased. Being present, honest and open becomes a hundred times more difficult because the smile will be sending soothing signals to your brain. You'll be effectively anesthetizing yourself to any of your real feelings. Your clown may be naturally enthusiastic and joyful, generally happy and willing to show it, but even so, certain negative situations will affect him/her. Emotional fluidity is crucial, so drop the social smile and smile only when you really feel genuine pleasure.

3. Being a good person

We've all had to learn how to be good; well behaved, polite, pleasant and thoughtful towards others. Unfortunately, being good can sometimes turn into a kind of straight jacket that disempowers us, annihilating our spontaneous self-expressive nature. "A good person" is caring and kind, *always*. As clowns, this (often unconscious) desire to please others, to be liked and accepted by one and all, leads to bland, wishy-washy behaviour. Nothing funny can happen if you're "a good person". Good people will automatically avoid conflict or creating waves (especially emotionally charged ones), they will apply sticking plasters to problems and not let anyone suffer, even if the suffering is play-acted within a clown improvisation. Good people will try to make everyone feel comfortable and loved.

There's nothing wrong with being a good person in life, in fact it's actually necessary for human survival, but if it's the only thing that defines you as a person, something *has* gone wrong. If you can't even *play* at being angry or evil, you're stuck in a mould and the fear of disapproval has won out over self-loyalty, self-confidence and self-esteem, all of which are essential requisites for clowning. Clowns know they will not be criticised for competing, rejecting, dominating, blaming or making fun of each other because it's all just a game... a game that's being played out for their and their audience's enjoyment.

Are you too good to be true?

Let's go back to waving at someone. This time wave and say "hello" to someone who's begun to get on your nerves. Try it now.

It's not the same as meeting a friend, is it? And meeting someone you're secretly but madly in love with will not be the same as meeting someone you find repulsive (and let's be honest, some people do repel you). Your mood will also affect any encounter you have; if you're feeling dark or down you'll react differently from when you're feeling tired and hungry.

So, since there are so many ways to respond to the world, does it make sense to always express goodness on stage? I'm not suggesting that you just turn it all around and be bad, but that you are honest about what's really going on for you. For instance, it's possible that when I asked you to wave again you didn't feel like it and so you didn't. This is a great reaction to have! On stage, as a clown, there isn't a "correct" way to react, even to the teacher. The choice of how to act or react depends only on you and what you think could be funny.

Bypassing self-defence mechanisms

You will by now have realised that The Good Clown's Handybook contains only self-defence mechanisms that are not at all helpful when learning clowning technique. There's a simple reason for this: clowns do not defend themselves. That is to say, clowns let things happen; they don't deny what they feel, they don't steer away from problem areas, they don't avoid failure, and they don't pretend to be able to deal with everything that comes their way. They're defenceless, innocent until they are proven guilty (and even then they will try to convince you of their innocence!). In fact, in their minds, everyone is innocent, except in the very moment they are proving they're not. Clowns have short-term memories; they don't walk around expecting the worst or constantly suspicious of others, and they are not fearful of showing their vulnerability; so they simply don't need protection.

In our highly "civilized" society it's almost impossible for us to feel safe without some kind of buffer. Only within our intimate circles of family or friends can we show how thin-skinned we feel at times, and sometimes, not even then. The truth is, it can be incredibly difficult to lay aside our armour and step out of our safe zone. If we look for synonyms of "defenceless" in a thesaurus, the long list of negative pronouns we find there goes a long way to explaining the reasons for this: helpless, unprotected, naked, powerless, endangered, exposed, unguarded, impotent. Doesn't make you want to leave your defences at home, does it?

But have you ever stopped to think what it is that you're protecting so ferociously and whether so many defences are actually necessary? Wouldn't it be liberating to let yourself be lighter, less concerned about what others may think or say? And wouldn't it be better not to take things so *personally* — to cultivate instead a sense of humour and of fun, be more generous about who you *really* are?

Your clown, by being defenceless, defends all the fundamentally important things to you:
- Your integrity
- Your singularity
- Your beliefs and values
- Your peculiarities
- Your emotional well-being
- Your personal strengths and abilities
- Your creativity
- Your right to make mistakes
- Your human solidarity

On stage the only serviceable defence that you have is your sense of humour. Actually, humour is normally the best option even off stage; it's frequently ingenious, generally appreciated and apt for all ages... don't leave home without it!

Take action!

If, while reading this chapter, you've realised that you've a secret copy of the Good Clown's Handbook (or part of one) stuffed in your head, congratulations! Now you can do something about it: get rid of all automatic, defensive behaviour whilst clowning by becoming aware of when you're not being honest and relaxed.

When improvising

During a clown workshop, when everything you're experiencing is either new or challenging — because even if you know the exercise you still have to meet the challenge of making your current improvisation work — you can easily set yourself the added goal of being fully present. In the safe environment of a course, where you're not expected to know everything, you can take moments to tune in to how you feel and what you would *really* like to do. You can listen to your body (are your gestures natural?), your breathing (are you breathing?), the tensions you feel (can you relax the parts that are tense?), the audience (are they with you? are you listening to them?).

If you think you do not feel anything, then be honest about your lack of feeling. As a teacher I'd rather a student said, "I don't feel anything" (which is one and the same thing as saying "I don't know what I feel") because I can then help them through their seeming lack of emotion. "How do you feel about not feeling anything? Do you feel panic, frustration, anger or maybe you don't give a damn?"

Sometimes it's necessary to jump start the connection with your senses because the truth is we're all human beings, so we're always feeling *something*! We have five senses to feel with; if one's not functioning properly we've still got four others sending us information. By the way, "I don't give a damn" is a defensive response, and as such part of the Handybook. However, as a clown you can play having a heart of stone if you're willing to exaggerate it. Eventually though, your clown will want to be vulnerable and open to the world. The sooner you let yourself experience how you feel and be fully alive, the more fun you both will have.

When performing

If you have already got a show or clown routine up and running then the best thing to do is film it and then take a critical look at your performance. Maybe you'll see where you need to make changes or maybe you'll want to appear less wooden. A great way to do either of these things is through *experiencing* your show again, getting back inside it and letting yourself play with it again. It's always a good thing to let your clown off the leash if things feel stale, allow him/her to try out something new. Maybe you just need to be more physically relaxed, do the whole show as if you've just smoked a joint or had a glass of wine! Be creative about the solutions you need to implement and let your audience be the barometer of how they're working.

On the street

Going out to play and practise on the street is a great way of shaking off any automatic reactions to people, situations, or even everyday objects. I've seen some radical changes occur in students who were having difficulties in the classroom when they were sent out to play on the street. Many thought they wouldn't be capable of putting on a red nose in the "normal" world but, after overcoming their resistance, were the ones who then wouldn't even take it off during the lunch break!

Out on the street you'll encounter endless stimulants for your creativity and also a real audience that will only play with you if you win them over. Obviously you don't have to make every passerby join in your game (some most definitely won't want to!) but if you'd like them to participate in some way, look them in the eyes and make sure they are willing. I ask my students not to over-react to people, not to impose on them discomfort of any kind, not to make them fearful. This is especially important when you're interacting with small children, who are particularly likely to freak out if you rush up to them wearing a red nose and shouting or gesticulaing wildly. Traumatic experiences with overbearing, grotesque clowns in childhood can produce a lifelong fear of clowns of any type. Psychologists have called this fear "coulrophobia" but what they and the sufferers haven't realised is that the real culprit is the Good Clown's Handybook, not the authentic clowns (whose work has for centuries had quite the opposite effect on their audiences' psychological health).

4
We're all ridiculous, even you!

Now that we've thrown the Good Clown's Handybook in the bin you'll be wanting to know what steps to take to enjoy your clown more fully and improve whatever technical knowledge of clowning you already have. My initial intention here was to give you a list of the all the basic techniques used by clowns, in a logical "first do this then do that" order, but I soon realised that this was impossible. It just doesn't work like that. The clown learning process is non-linear; one person will first need to assimilate one aspect of the technique, whilst someone else will need to start with quite another. Therefore, the following set of guide-lines is actually more useful: Be authentic. Play. Express what you feel. Share with your audience. Have problems. Be foolish. Be interested. Think simple. Fail. Be vulnerable. Apply your sense of humour. Exaggerate. Feel the comic beats. Repeat successes. Enjoy yourself. Give in to temptation. Be honest. Step over the boundaries. Rediscover the world. Be stupid.

The art of clowning may look like child's play but I warn you now that assimilating all of these guide-lines will take time and dedication. Knowing and understanding how each one works is not the same as putting them into practice in front of an audience. Performing is also the only real way of knowing where your strengths and weaknesses lie. You'll find that you can do certain things without thinking while others will take a conscious effort to master. Live performance will give you the opportunity of exploring the universe your clown moves in — what your clown is capable of, how s/he expresses him/herself, what s/he wants to communicate, what games attract him/her, etc. — as well as giving you the chance to investigate the ways you can put into practice each guide-line.

It is, however, useful to know the underlying reasons for each of the clown guide-lines listed above and their individual technical, philosophical and psychological aspects. As this involves a lot of interesting and important material I've divided it up. Each chapter will tackle at least one guide-line but some are so related that I thought they were best explained within the same frame of reference, so you'll find these treated in the same chapter. You can either dive in where you feel you are most stuck or follow the chapters in their given order. But I would recommend first making sure you know you are ridiculous, as it is an absolutely indispensible first step.

Yes, you are ridiculous, we all are, maybe not all of the time but most of the time! Consequently in clowning, what you really have to learn is how to recognise and skillfully expose all the comic elements you already have at your disposal. Developing these aspects and consolidating a sense of humour (not only capable of creating laughter but also of opening up people's hearts and minds) depends on how much you are able to just be yourself. In other words, how willing you are to be authentically *you*.

Being authentic

A few years ago I had a student who was a professional stunt man. "This is fantastic!" he told the group at the end of the first day, "It feels as if the less I do, the more people laugh. In fact, if I try to do something impressive or planned, nobody reacts to the ideas I've had. They laugh when I'm not doing anything at all. So I've decided to carry on doing nothing, how simple!"

Obviously the "I'm not doing anything" was how he experienced his performances but he was of course doing something on stage, and doing it with verve. He was giving us a delightful display of authenticity. He was being himself so completely and genuinely that he had us beguiled. While the rest of his group struggled with themselves to feel what they wanted to do, he simply did it. Having no complexes about himself, he followed his heart, and even though this could lead him into difficulties, he had enough faith in his own resourcefulness to know it could be relied on to save the moment. We laughed because his sparkling, charismatic ridiculousness filled us with joy. He, on the other hand, found no difficulty in acting on impulse, taking risks and finding ingenious solutions to the problems that arose, because these traits were second nature to him. Clowning seemed easy compared to jumping off buildings or being dragged around by a horse!

So, when you're just being yourself something singular and fascinating is bound to happen. If you're not worrying about what others might think of you, you'll allow yourself to have fun, you will do or express whatever you want to, and because you're not holding back on anything, you'll act on impulse and speak your mind. This state of inner freedom means you allow the unexpected to happen. You'll undoubtedly do silly things, make mistakes or find yourself in awkward situations, but you'll also tap into your genius and your charm. An open, sincere person is difficult to resist. You may not think this but everyone has charisma — some part of their personality that, transmitted through the clown frequency, will draw others to them. When you're on stage as a clown, *you* are the show. The less preoccupied you are by this fact, the better you and your show will be.

Being authentic means being honest. Honestly then, who are you?

There seem to be so many answers to this question that most people wonder where on earth to begin. That's because who we are is a complex issue. We have so many different "me" identities:

the "me" of my personal data (name, age, address), the biological me (my sex, genes, medical history), the professional me (your curriculum vitae), the social me, the intimate me, the spiritual me, the unconscious me, the me I pretend to be, the me I think I am, and the me's of my different developmental stages (inner child, adolescent, young adult, etc.).

Who then, is the real "me"??

Finding your true self can be challenging, but the red nose will help immensely. Once you have it on the real you will slip out. The red nose is a mask, the smallest mask that exists, but as such, it's the one that reveals the most; it unmasks the person who wears it. If you remain open-minded about who you are, right now, in the present moment, you'll be pleasantly surprised on stage. You'll soon discover when the authentic you is running wild because the audience will be glued to their seats and laughing!

"When clowning, I try not to let what I think I am
get in the way of all I can be."
Virginia Imaz, clown, Spain

Being authentic, however, is not always pretty or nice. There'll be comic parts of your personality that will be real eye openers, others will be like old friends, others you will deny or reject. Welcome them all! Accepting everything that spontaneously arises is part of the clown's job description. Many of my students are amazed by how enthusiastic, creative or unencumbered they can be as a clown. But it's a fact that vitality is an innate human quality. The closer you are to your natural state of being the more vital you'll feel. Every time you go out on stage you have a new opportunity to show yourself and your audience what you're made of, and you'll stand a better chance of impressing them when you stop trying to impress them.

> "Being funny is not only an innate talent. I've been dedicated to comedy for many years and experience has taught me that humour can be continuously developed and defined by exploring our inner self, with the goal of finding our self confidence. I think that the authentic comic talent lies in one's core essence."
>
> *Leo Bassi, clown/buffon, Italy*

Fun versus seriousness

Deep down we'd all like to feel free enough to consistently be ourselves in all situations; but the truth is, we don't find it easy. At some point in our lives, the majority of us chose what we thought was a more presentable, acceptable version of ourselves, which effectively meant repressing a certain aspect or aspects of our personality. These days people can even choose to change their physical appearance. We can literally cut away parts of ourselves we don't like and become the fantasy person we've dreamt about being. In short, we don't live in a culture that encourages either outer or inner self-acceptance. Nonetheless, we still all aspire to the goal of personal freedom, we all have a deep down desire to be unconstrained, uninhibited, and unhampered by censure or convention.

I now receive many students who, rather than coming to my courses to learn clown technique, come in search of some lost part of themselves. They come to find their joy, vitality, expressiveness, sense of humour, peace of mind, etc. And what they unearth within themselves are not merely these qualities, but a whole universe of inverted values. Their clown reveals a lost world, a world where comedy and fun run amok. It's a world that can only be reached through their constant ability to laugh at their most sacred possession: themselves — or more precisely, the identity they fabricated around themselves.

It really is such a great tragicomedy that human beings take themselves so very seriously. We all possess this firm, mad belief in our own importance, in the importance of all our actions, feelings and desires. We also believe that such obsessive self importance is a sign of adulthood (when in actual fact it's a sure sign of lack of maturity). An adult who seeks fun in life is generally considered frivolous and irresponsible, not someone whose feet are firmly on the ground. Real adults face the seriousness of life, they take themselves seriously and teach their children to be serious. But where did this notion come from, that to be an adult you have to be deadly serious about yourself? And why is its opposite, fun, now reserved only for leisure activities (on which we spend less and less of our time)?

"Yes, I am an adult, but this doesn't mean that I have to lose sight of adventure, beauty or pleasure.

As an adult I can feel, play, share with others and remain interested in everything around me."
David Berga, clown, Catalonia

Obviously there are many serious things happening in the world that one can't take lightly — such as war, hunger or poverty. But it is worrying that, as adults, we habitually respond to the thousands of stimuli we receive from life with poker-faced humourlessness. This lack of a humorous response should be treated like a virus within us. If we don't find a cure for it we will, without a doubt, fall *serious*-ly ill sooner or later. Often, all the cure we need is a change of perspective on the uncomfortable thing that is happening to us. Just remove the "This is important" label we unwittingly stuck on it. Clowns can do this without thinking; their detachment is possible because their gaze is not fixed on their own navels. Clowns see the wider picture; they see the underlying comedy of our tragic human plight.

The first clowns to appear on film (Charlie Chaplin, Buster Keaton, the Marx Brothers, etc.) have become absolute classics of their time and their films are still widely appreciated and enjoyed. There are also many traditional clown routines being performed today that haven't lost their ability to provoke amusement or delight in modern audiences. But why are the films and routines so popular still? Well, apart from being created by imaginative and talented artists, they have two other common denominators that are universally therapeutic; they all offer us a comic vision of the unfortunate, difficult, and precarious situation we humans find ourselves in and they've all placed human nature under a microscope to show it to us just as it is. And what a crazy bunch of situations we can find ourselves in without even trying! Absurd, irrational, surreal, excessive, incongruous, incoherent situations, but all part of living on earth. And how ridiculous can we get when faced with these crazy situations! Yes, we've all experienced the human plight, we're all human; but clowns just see the funny side and transform it into art.

> "Humour is proof of our human maturity."
> *Carles Sans, Cía. El Tricicle, Spain*

The professional clowns I know don't spend every waking minute having fun and being funny. Certainly they enjoy themselves, but they're also committed to their work, which means being serious about their professional responsibilities. They have to create, sell and perform their shows without losing their sense of humour. Seriousness and fun can compliment one another. Taking seriously the things that you're passionate about and having fun with life's difficulties and your own mad behaviour will improve your overall quality of life. It's a question of finding the balance that's healthy for you.

Children as a source of inspiration

Alex Navarro, who is as passionate about clowns as I am, has also spent years investigating the art of clowning. He has a theory that cannot be proved, but makes complete sense: that traditional clowns found a wealth of comic inspiration in children and used much of what they found funny about them in their routines.

Maybe you're not surprised to read this. Children can be hilarious because they're absolutely prepared to make a spectacle of themselves. In their innocence they express how they feel, what they want or what they've learnt, which more often than not is exaggerated, confused or limited, yet filled with imagination. Not long ago I saw a mother and child walking in the street, and while the mother was walking forwards in a straight line without even noticing her surroundings, her son was hanging from her arm, balancing on the very edge of the pavement as he jogged along. His free arm was splayed out as if he was flying in an aeroplane dodging imaginary bullets from enemies attacking on all sides. His whole body took part in the illusion he was creating, he was the hero of the moment, invincible. His action-packed experience made me laugh out loud, all that vitality and creativity brimming over the pavement was heart-warmingly funny.

The traditional clowns no doubt made mental notes of all the best gags they saw children "performing". My daughter for instance, when she was only sixteen months old, spontaneously started doing gags that celebrated clowns from the last century popularized in their performances. Alex wrote down a couple of them:

> At the time we were living next to an olive grove and one day I took Amara for a walk through the grove. She started picking up the fallen olives until both her hands were full. Then one of the olives she held fell to the ground. On bending to pick it up, more of the olives she had in her hands fell to the ground. She looked up at me and then tried again to pick up the fallen olives, only instead she let others fall from her grasp. Her persistence was astounding, again and again she tried and failed to pick up all the olives. Watching her reminded me of the classic clown gag with a sheaf of paper, where clowns pick up dropped papers in an ever more desperate and crazy routine.

The other gag happened at home. We had blown up a few balloons for her to play with and I asked her to bring me one. She went to fetch it but on reaching the balloon she accidentally kicked it out of her reach. She looked at me with surprise, as if the balloon had moved of its own accord, magically. Then she went for a different one... and another... and another... each time accidentally kicking the balloon away. It was as funny as watching the classic gag that many clowns use, kicking their fallen hat out of reach just as they are attempting to pick it up.

Over time, clowns have learnt to skillfully make use of the best moments in childhood. That's why it now seems as if small children are imitating the professional clowns and not visa versa! I'll explain in greater detail all the parallels and differences between clowns and children in the relevant sections but before leaving this one I'd like to underline the easy-to-tap-into comedy resource available to you whenever you spend time with children. Here are just three anecdotes of the many I have heard from friends with kids:

Edith, five years old, was sitting on a beach with her mother when a plane flew overhead with a publicity banner trailing behind. "That's a brand new aeroplane," said Edith, "It's so new it's still got the label on it".

Philip, five years old, visited a farm with his parents for the first time. He wandered off for a short while only to come running back full of excitement. He opened his hands to show an egg, "Look what the hen just pooed!" he said happily.

Laura, four years old, was taken to the doctor's by her father for a vaccine jab. The doctor kindly asked her which arm she used most. She turned to her father, "Why does he want to know that?" Her father replied, "So he can inject you in the other one." She blinked once before saying, "I use them both equally, can we go now?"

5
Clarity and simplicity

"A clown adores being seen, adores the pleasure of having an audience. He knows that the moment won't last, that when it's over he'll have to leave the spotlight, so he'll give his all because of that, because he has been given a space to be a spectacle."
Pablo Luengas, laughter doctor, Mexico

In conventional theatre productions the actors move in a fictitious reality that doesn't include being watched by an audience. In clown performances the opposite occurs, the crowd is always acknowledged and included, never ignored. Clowns see, hear and react to their audiences, even when performing in conventional theatre spaces. They deliberately draw everyone into the action; sometimes inviting them to be active participants in their stage play, either from where they sit or stand together or as individuals on the stage with them.

Certainly, clowns developed their art under very different circumstances from theatrical actors; working in open public spaces and circus arenas required an altogether different style of performance and presentation. The audiences that clowns faced were from every social class, often rowdy and vociferous; impossible, in fact, to ignore! However, the openness of clowns to the presence of the audience and their use of direct eye contact perhaps has more to do with their understanding of the nature of laughter than the spaces worked in or audiences they performed for.

What's so funny?

Often, beginner clown students feel an enormous pressure to do something the moment they get out on stage. It's as if they're suddenly struck by a sense of urgency; something, anything has got to happen *immediately*. As a result, they tend to shift straight into compulsive action and can't seem to be able to change gear, even though what they're doing isn't working at all. Movement becomes a shield to hide behind or a defence against possible criticism; at least they can't be accused of not trying!

When, however, they begin to relax and find their feet, they realise that their movement can be orchestrated to obtain specific results. They also discover that pausing for a moment or two, especially when they first appear, is actually advantageous. It gives them time to connect — with the atmosphere, the space, and the elements that could prove useful (objects, noises, physical sensations); but, above all, with their audience. A pause of this kind can be very brief — it will often be simply a matter of taking a breath, or releasing one. This is often all they need to become grounded and present.

The audience also enjoys the pause in movement, it gives them time to absorb the clown's arrival. People love being given the chance to make an initial appraisal of any newcomer. They want to know who has just entered and what they might be doing there. Experienced clown students know that the first impressions they create can really get the ball rolling and by simply doing nothing they can achieve a great deal.

"Doing nothing" as a clown is not the "doing nothing" of ordinary life. On stage, not *doing* means the emphasis is on *being*. Walking out to meet an audience is not like walking into a corner shop or taking a stroll through your local park, it requires you to feel a sense of aliveness and alertness that surpasses the day to day. This heightened state of being is similar to the way you might feel when leaving your hotel for the first time, the day you arrive in an exotic, unknown country. This kind of *being* is electric, it captures other people's attention, draws them in and affects them, as if they too have somehow been plugged into the same frequency. If you've ever fallen in love you'll know what I'm talking about. Somehow your joy and heightened sense of attractiveness is infectious. As you walk around newly aware of all the reasons you have to be happy, miraculously everywhere you look, someone's smiling back at you. When creating humour this feeling of inner vitality is essential, its waves can break up other people's states of boredom, distraction or apathy in an instant.

Evidently, as a clown you can enter the stage in a thousand different ways, and express any emotion you feel inclined to. There's no golden rule, only a fact; that something new is happening. This starting point should be your presentation card as this is when the audience will form their all important first opinion of you. Within a few seconds they'll take everything about you into account; your clothing, bearing, mannerisms, overall appearance, even your personal charm. And the opinion they form of you will either help or hinder you, it will either awaken their interest or make them wary of you.

Creating a feeling of proximity with your audience is one of the keys to successful clowning. As a clown you can make this happen without them even knowing how you did it. Through simply recognizing their presence and openly

inviting them to observe you, you'll have automatically initiated them into a relationship that offers intimacy, and if you
then show them who you are, with clarity and transparency,
you'll have effectively offered them a bond of trust. From
there, establishing a friendly alliance won't be hard at all.

Recent scientific studies have proven beyond doubt that
laughter is a highly contagious social phenomenon. There
now exists a bulk of data that certifies that adults rarely laugh
when alone, that it's only when we interact socially that our
humour gets triggered to any degree, and that the deeper the
emotional bond we share the more heartily we'll laugh together. All these studies have simply confirmed what clowns
already knew. That's why sharing has always played an important role in their performances. As laughter "scientists",
they discovered centuries ago that the more they share and
acknowledge, the greater the bond created with their audience, and the heartier the laughter that's generated there.

Timing

As I have said, the relationship a clown aspires to is warm,
open and friendly. Baffling behaviour would therefore be
totally counter-productive because confusion creates distance
between human beings and confused people don't laugh.
Clowns have therefore developed communication strategies
that are grounded in the principles of simplicity and clarity.
They know how important it is not to overload the audience
with information or demand too much on an intellectual
level; no-one should have to struggle to understand what's
going on or why something's happening. Consequently, clowns
have become skilled in offering manageable portions of stage
play, in timing their actions or reactions using personalized
rhythms and in providing the vital intervals in which comedy
and laughter flourish.

"The ability of the clown must be the ability to simplify, to reduce the complexity of reality to something very simple. It's actually much easier to be complicated."

Gardi Hutter, clown, Switzerland

All clowns have a highly personal internal rhythmn that emerges from their natural way of being and doing. A highly strung person will have a faster on-stage rhythm than a relaxed, easy going person. Alongside these variable personal rhythmns, all clowns must also learn the skill of "comic timing", which means how to use rhythm to create maximum comic impact. The pacing of gags entails fine tuning the senses to recognise the perfect moment to gesticulate, react or deliver the punch line. It's a skill that's usually honed through physical and vocal precision training but some people seem to have a gift and do it absolutely naturally.

As comedy is often lurking just under the surface of most mundane daily events, clowns pay strict attention to detail when performing. In consequence, their actions mark a series of beats, accenting each detail that is given focus. Generally, the tempo they adopt is slower than the one we ordinarily use in daily life. This enables the audience to more easily "read" what's going on, but it works to the clown's advantage too. In an improvisation, pacing the action will give clowns the time to assimilate things that happen and share how they feel about them, and, if something works, they'll be able to play even more of the details. The tempo that's adopted is therefore vital to creating comic situations.

Normally, in everyday life, when we're confronted with a problem, we immediately attempt to solve it. Or, if someone gives us a pleasant surprise, we feel happy straight away.

Likewise, if a stranger makes an odd gesture in our direction, we quickly decide to ignore it. But, for a clown, reacting so instantaneously to any of these situations would mean abruptly putting an end to a possible game; the game of having a problem, or the game of doubting the true nature of a gift, or the game of misinterpreting an innocent gesture. All these games are open-ended possibilities for fun. Whilst keeping within the original framework for the game, the clowns can play freely. An important part of this play will involve the rhythmic games that provoke laughter; the acceleration or deceleration of movement, the length or timing of the pauses, the tempo fluctuations of the differing emotional states, etc.

Professional clowns are well aware of the importance of their comic timing. If the correct timing is not observed, a gag will lose its impact or it'll look false and will therefore not get a laugh. A new gag will usually be given a "trial period", in which the timing is fine-tuned so that eventually the gag will always work. The most common tendency in beginners is to accelerate, to do everything too quickly, but doing things too slowly can be equally devastating. There's always a specific timing for each gag, action or reaction, and either you instinctively feel it or you have to work with it until you do.

The pauses

In my workshops I encourage my students to use different rhythms in their improvisations; to play with the beats, to work at the comic timing of their gags, to listen to the audience's need for a change of tempo, but, above all, to understand the immense value of the pause. As I've said, pauses enable information to be both given and received, so the length of the pause held is determined as much by the situation a clown finds him/herself in as by the reaction s/he is receiving from the audience; but generally a pause will last between two or three seconds. Below, you'll find some examples of the kind of information that can be conveyed through the pauses in a clown performance.

A clown crosses the stage and accidentally knocks over a small table with a very expensive looking vase he'd failed to notice. As the vase crashes to the floor it breaks into several pieces. The clown freezes.

Information conveyed: He's heard the crash and asks himself, "What was that?"

He looks at the broken vase on the floor. Pause.

Information: He realises that there are pieces of porcelain on the floor and that his clumsiness is to blame.

He looks at the audience, his eyes opening wide. Pause.

Information: There are witnesses to his action. He feels exposed.

He looks down at the broken vase again then fearfully at the audience. Pause.

Information: He knows he's got to remedy the situation but can't think how.

He notices a rug downstage and has an idea. He pretends to see dirt on the rug, giving him the perfect excuse to shake it wildly in the air. He then places it neatly over the broken vase. Pause.

Information: He thinks that he's cleverly solved the problem.

He looks at the audience with satisfaction. Pause.

Information: He's got nothing to worry about now.

He exits the stage.

Through the pauses, clowns are able to communicate clearly everything that is happening; not just what's going on superficially but all their inner thoughts and emotions. Contrary to what you might expect, pauses can actually breathe life into stage action. Since the clown remains fully alive when holding them, keeping his/her energy focused and present, the moment is *lived*. The clown never loses his/her interest in what's going on and thereby the audience gets sucked in too. They quickly realise that the clown lives in a world that is neither boring nor limited, that every moment is a moment where anything could happen, and what does is often a complete surprise. And yet they instinctively understand that they can still relax and laugh if they feel like it, without fearing that in doing so they'll miss out on something. The clown will pause, and let them laugh before continuing with the show.

6
Clown language

Clowns have had to find a universally comprehensible language to use in their performances. With audiences of varied ages, classes and cultures they needed a form of communication that was able to transmit information clearly and effectively, a common language that could be seen, read and understood the world over. Fortunately, just such a language was being practised daily, right in front of their eyes.

Small children may have a limited vocabulary, but they always find a way of being understood. Their methods are straightforward: unembarrassed honesty, unabashed creativity, and, more often than not, disarming playfulness.

Clowns saw how effective such techniques could be, both as a way to truly get a message across but also as a way to have fun at the same time. They therefore incorporated and developed these same methods in their art; fine tuning the style, tone and delivery without losing the essential qualities of spontaneity and authenticity.

It's not surprising then that clown students often find they have to reverse the effects that education and adulthood have had on their communication skills. Uninhibited physical, emotional and verbal expression is paramount in clowning. In order once again to be a master communicator it's important to unearth your former skills, recover your unique ways of expression and recapture the pleasure of playfulness.

Non-verbal communication

Children spontaneously practise their communication skills from a very young age. Knowing how to communicate their needs and interpret the information that they receive is crucial to their survival. Babies are born with the ability to cry and smile, and at the same time are sensitive to different faces, voices and physical contact. Non-verbal communication is essential in all the first stages of human development, but its impact and importance remains powerful even in adult communication. Studies realised in 1972 by the psychologist Albert Mehrabian, about the relative importance of verbal and non-verbal messages, concluded that the actual words an orator used influenced the listener only 7%, while the tone of voice did so 38%, and the body language 55% (body language includes gestures, facial expressions, physical posture and eye contact).

Anthropologists have studied human behaviour in many different cultures and, while they found many differences, they were eventually able to identify several "human universals"; behaviour that was intrinsically similar regardless of race, sex or culture. Amongst other things they discovered that all humans innately study the body language of other human beings. Worldwide, we all observe with a keen interest other people's faces. The basic emotions have specific facial expressions that are recognised throughout the world, and we're all particularly skilled in distinguishing between an honest or dishonest emotional expression.

So, whether you are conscious of it or not, you are an expert in reading, interpreting and appraising non-verbal communication. All humans are. Clowns just make use of this universal expertise. They know that a sudden widening of the eyes communicates they're shocked or surprised, that holding the breath will show they're scared, or that briefly hunching their shoulders helps express incomprehension. Experienced clowns use their bodies as consciously as trained actors do, knowing that even the subtlest movements are capable of communicating very specific things. They do not have to illustrate (by the excessive use of gestures or unnecessary physical explanations), because their intentions can be easily communicated through efficient natural gestures. For example, if they want their audience to understand that they must go but would rather stay, they simply look towards the exit, then look at their audience, then heave a sigh of resignation before walking slowly off stage.

Find the physical games

Although clowns know how and when to use their natural body movements when communicating, this obviously doesn't stop them from hamming things up, from making movements that are exaggerated, extravagant or stylized. It's in their nature to entertain both themselves and others by playing different physical games but there are also two very good reasons for doing so; 1. eccentric movement can be extremely funny and, 2. being so similar in appearance to the physical games small children play, it allows clowns to break all the social rules and not have their audience turn against them for doing so.

1. Eccentric movement

Eccentric movement can be observed daily in children between the ages of one and five. As they do not have complete control over their bodies they're prone to making odd or absurd physical movements. Having no notions of time or responsibilities, or of what is valuable, dirty, fragile or dangerous, they are completely open and responsive to their five senses. Their actions, unchecked by mental interferences, are often motivated by the stimuli provided by their sensations. They can be egocentric, stubborn, impulsive and messy; all without self judgement.

During these early stages of development, exploration is the order of the day, but by degrees they become aware of the ways in which older children and adults are using their bodies. Their desire to imitate the activities of their elders then pushes them to try out new movements, but without the fully formed musculature necessary to complete such actions, their bodies almost always fail them. Fortunately, they're both inventive and determined. They'll turn what they want to learn into a game and happily practise the same set of movements over and over again.

Clowns will imitate any of these behavioural patterns when it suits their needs. Individual bodies have their own possibilities and limitations. Limbs and articulations can play great games, individually or in combination, and each gesture can be graduated in energy or intensity from the delicate to the daring. Sometimes though, they'll simply give their body free reign to play whatever feels right, allowing movements to be created or re-created on the spot. This gives their actions an absolutely natural quality, even if they're made up of some very unnatural movements.

At other times they'll return to the classic games of:

- getting absorbed in the physical pleasure of any given movement (or series of movements), repeating it every which way until the momentary madness abates.
- losing control over a part or parts of their body, or over an object they're using.
- taking a small inconsequential movement and exaggerating it bit by bit, either making it larger or longer (through extension or slow motion) or at the other extreme, making it smaller or faster.
- imitation. They'll either play up the parody of an authority figure or they'll attempt to demonstrate the actions of their heroes, however unconvincingly!

2. Breaking the social rules

Small children are happily unaware of the social rules that govern interpersonal adult behaviour. They can stare at whoever they like for as long as they like, leave half-chewed pastries in our hands, insult us with the truth (along the lines of "Why is your nose so big?"), scream in our ears, invade our personal space, not listen to our commands — and we, the adults, are still inclined to forgive them; we'll smile at them lovingly at the end of the day. Why? Because they're innocent. Their actions may inconvenience us, but they don't intimidate us. The fact is that when we're alone with them we suddenly feel so much freer to express ourselves than when we are in the company of adults. We'll pull silly faces, make stupid sounds, and generally act stupidly, and because we know they're not judging us, we also maintain a similar mental openness. We allow them much more freedom of action and reaction than we would normally be comfortable with and we also give them much more of our attention.

It's hardly surprising then that clowns have also adopted the characteristic innocence that accompanies even the most outrageous behaviour in small children. This one quality alone allows them much more physical freedom. They become exempt from all the constraining social rules, such as:

- eye contact between people that are strangers should only last one and a half seconds. (Children only learn to break eye contact at the age of four or five).
- people's personal space should be respected. (Children only become aware of this concept around the age of four).
- permission is required before touching other people's things (usually assimilated by children around the age of four or five).

Clowns will stare at people, invade their personal space, open their handbags and pick their pockets, but rarely does anyone protest. In fact, audiences have come to expect a certain amount of unlicensed behaviour from clowns, so they may even encourage you to go further than you thought possible!

What if...

So, at least to start with, the art of physical game-playing is more about journeying backwards than forwards. In order to find the game that creates "the show", you first have to loosen up your body and investigate your own physical expressivity. More often than not, the games that really work originate from your natural gestures, the peculiarities of your physical structure, the movements you get pleasure from performing, and the way you normally use your body to communicate your overt or subtle messages.

Before leaping into action it's important to be aware of what your body is transmitting, even in its neutral state. Do you know what your body is communicating to other people? What do they perceive when they look at you?

Your body is of course, absolutely singular, as is the way you walk, gesticulate, sit, etc. And, however many times you may have studied yourself in the mirror, you will never have seen reflected there what another person sees. Many of my students are taken aback by the imitations other students do of them in class. They don't recognise their own physical presence. They've never realised that they move one arm much more than the other when walking or that they have so much rigidity in their torso, or that right beneath the surface of their studied coolness, it's obvious to one and all that they're a push over! Even people who have trained their bodies in other disciplines (dancers, actors, gymnasts, etc.) aren't necessarily aware of the information their body is projecting on stage. Also, as I've said, the red nose reveals more than it masks, it exposes intrinsic physical characteristics and these are magnified by being on stage. It may seem surprising, but almost everyone needs to receive feedback for a while, to help them see themselves exactly as they are and begin to assimilate what they are communicating corporally.

Physical games can most easily be initiated by paying attention to the senses. At first, the novelty of each performance experience may push your five senses into hyperactivity, creating a deluge of information that is almost impossible to process. So, during your initial training period, you'll need to learn how to give each sense individual attention. Paying attention to any of them can provide you with a physical game to play: an aroma that takes you back down memory lane, the touch of a hand that creates endless body spasms, a light that leaves you blinded, etc. The most basic sense game is 'What If... ?' It works like this:

> *What if... I stuck my tongue out and felt it, not as a gesture with a connotation but simply as a fat tongue. What if... I felt the tension at its root, the cold air caressing the end of it? What if... I pushed it out further, explored the full extent of its possibilities? What if... I tried to smell it, taste it or see it? What if... I added sound AND lateral movement? What if... I try more complicated combinations of movement? What if... I grab it between my fingers and try to talk?*

Letting your body play creatively and recovering your natural physical spontaneity is an essential first step. But this is not something to practise as a dancer would, looking for beauty and ever more incredible physical abilities. Clowns search for what is ridiculous, or just plain funny; and this could be some amazing physical feat or just a tiny pursing of the lips.

"In physical comedy more skill does not necessarily mean it will be funnier — it's how you use it. I think there is a danger in fact in using too much skill because you have to make it fit. In comedy you're always trying to make things look believable, within whatever style you're doing, even in a stylized clown routine. More than skill one should think in terms of exposure to possibilities. Cultivating a sense of where you might go with something is fundamental."

John Towsen, physical comedy teacher, U.S.A.

Fortunately, there are already some excellent books on physical comedy, not to mention the vast legacy of information to be found in both vintage and modern day films. Slapstick (mock violence), silly walks, eccentric dance moves, playing with objects in odd ways and physical "business", are all part of a grand theatrical tradition that dates back to the commedia dell'arte. I definitely recommend you make use of the information that's available and experiment for yourself the different techniques. By way of encouragement I'll leave you with another piece of John Towsen's knowledge:

"One has to play with gag structures. Part of the gag is physical, another part is psychological — what's going on in the characters mind. Also the timing is very important — you have to take into account what rhythms you've used before, because you don't want to repeat the exact same rhythm every time. You play with the audience, with their expectations. The last thing you want is that your audience is ahead of you."

The emotional content

I remember my daughter, at the age of four, furiously denying that she was at all tired when it came to her bedtime, night after night after night. The signs of her fatigue would be as clear as day; she'd start talking like a baby and yet force her eyes wide open as if she were trying to fool me into believing how awake she was. If I tried to point out that she was in fact sleepy she'd shout at me angrily, "No, I'm NOT, I am NOT tired!" and then burst into tears before hiding under the nearest cushion. As a clown I couldn't help but secretly appreciate her theatrical attempts to avoid going to bed even though, as a mother, her truly ridiculous performances didn't fool me in the slightest.

Having spent a lot of time with small children, I've found many parallels in the ways that they and clowns express their emotions; though obviously clowns are the experts in dramatic form and comic content, whereas children are just the gifted amateurs. Small children are unable to be deceitful about the way they feel, even if, as with my daughter, they endeavour to be. However, they can also be acutely aware of the influence that their emotional expressions have on others. This keeps them adjusting and perfecting their expressive competence. Mostly, they're trying to attain maximum leverage, especially with adults, in order to get what they think they need. So, if they aren't getting the reaction they seek, they'll pump up the volume or be more insistent or, if that fails, they'll try moving closer, stand on a chair or even throw something at you! They are, in fact, extremely creative and sometimes this can be very comical.

One day, while walking through town, I heard a child wailing inconsolably. It sounded as if something terrible had happened or as if he was in some great physical pain, but when I went to find out if I could be of any help, I saw the child was fine. He was firmly planted in front of his father with his arms stretching upwards. This scandalously dramatic behaviour was all just a desperate attempt to get his father to carry him! I had to laugh. I could remember such feelings myself: the overwhelming sensation of fatigue, the enticing pleasure of being carried, the frustration of not being listened to and the tantalizing satisfaction of getting one's own way.

It's easy to see why clowns mimic the emotional patterns of small children; why they consciously apply these patterns in their performances. Nevertheless, the amount of empathetic or comic juice they're able to squeeze from them is always governed by their astuteness of choice. Choosing how or when to stretch out, exaggerate or play down an emotional reaction is an art. In an improvisation, clowns will react to events in accordance with their gut feelings (honest reactions get the greatest laughs); but that's just the first step. They then need to exploit the reaction, transform it into a game that will keep the laughter flowing. Clowns don't try to convince their audience that they're really sad or angry or in love. The comedy (especially with regard to the "negative" emotions: fear, jealousy, sadness, etc.) lies in the obviousness of the game. Clowns play at being provoked emotionally, they'll react and get involved with the expression of their feelings, but they'll exchange one emotion for another just as soon as they realise that they're not getting the reaction they're looking for from the audience, or, if something more interesting occurs to them.

Revel in feeling
There are many ways to represent the emotions when clowning; but this has more to do with personal style than a concrete technique. I recommend you find ways to express all the emotions playfully, and expand your range within each one. It's helpful to see the emotions as musical scales: find your maximum and minimum expressions and all that is in

between. Run up and down the scale, using all the notes, or maybe sometimes missing out a few, but never making huge irrational leaps from emotion to emotion without a logical motivation. Our emotional states have a reason for being, if you don't let the audience know why you're suddenly sad when half a second ago you were happy, they'll get confused and you'll have lost them. So make sure they know the reason for your sudden change of heart. Did you see something that broke it, find out you were penniless, or think of something tragic?

Having said this, I should clarify a few points. Some people find it difficult to express certain emotions; they'll feel at ease with joy, for example, but uncomfortable with anger, or they simply won't be able to find ways to play being scared, or sad. It's worth respecting your emotional baselines (the emotions that come naturally and are expressed with ease) because you'll undoubtedly get more laughs using them than the ones that feel artificial. Your natural emotional expressiveness will also influence your clown's ability to play the scales of individual emotions, especially the highest and lowest notes. If you habitually use subtle or light tones in normal life, you will be able to use these same tones on stage to great effect. It may never be necessary for you to go overboard or use exaggerated tones to get a laugh. However, it's important to remember that your clown is always emotionally generous. S/he holds nothing back, even with perfect strangers.

"I have realised that all the influences of my life, from childhood onwards, have resurfaced in my work. Everything that I have lived and felt are now my clown's primary source of inspiration."
Carlo Mô, clown, Spain

Vocal freedom

Traditional clowns used their natural wit and a wide variety of word play (malapropisms, rhyming slang, spoonerisms, and puns) to create some very funny dialogues. A few have survived. The following dialogue, between a Whiteface and an Auguste, was entrusted to me by Manel Vallès (Totó) just before he died in 2011. He began his clowning career in 1949 (at the age of fourteen) and was a professional for sixty-two years.

> WHITEFACE: Do you know what philosophy is? *(the Auguste nods his head)* What would you extract from it?
>
> AUGUSTE: I'd extract two girlfriends, Philo for you and Sofie for me!
>
> W: No, no. Listen, using philosophy, I can prove that you're not here.
>
> A: What?! Of course I'm here, and I'm not budging.
>
> W: Well, I'm going to demonstrate, beyond a shadow of a doubt, that you aren't here.
>
> A: Oh, yeah? Go on then.
>
> W: But first let's make a bet. I'll put down five pounds, so you put down five too. If I demonstrate that you're not here I win, if not, then you win.

A: Ok.

W: Right then. Are you in Madrid?

A: No, I'm here.

W: Well then, if you're not in Madrid you must be in Santander.

A: No, not in Madrid or in Santander, I'm right here and I'm staying right here *(looking at the money)*.

W: So then you must be in Seville.

A: You mean you must be in Sant Boi! *(in Sant Boi there used to a very well known mental hospital)*.

W: Just answer my question!

A: Of course I'm not in Seville!

W: So, you're not in Madrid, or in Santander or in Seville. That means that you are somewhere else.

A: Of course.

W: You've lost then, because you've just admitted you're somewhere else! *(He picks up the money)*.

A: Ha, very clever! Hey, hey, wait a minute, let's do it again. Let's bet.

W: Ok, here's my five.

A: I'll bet five too *(but instead of putting down another five pound note he picks up the one the Whiteface put down)*. And I bet five more *(he puts down the note he just picked up)*.

W: Ok, five more, and I raise you another five *(he puts down ten pounds)*.

A: Ok, another five *(he pretends to place another bet but instead picks up all the money and pockets it)*. This time I'll ask the questions.

W: Fine, it's all the same to me *(but he's thinking "what a fool!")*

A: Are you in Madrid?

W: No, I'm not in Madrid.

A: Are you in Santander?

W: No, I'm right here, can't you see me?

A: Are you in Seville?

W: Of course not! Not in Madrid, Santander or Seville.

A: Are you saying that you're somewhere else?

W: No, I'm here. You've lost. The money's mine *(he looks for the banknotes)*. Hey! Where's the cash? *(he realises what must have happened)*. You've taken it!

A: It wasn't me!

W: Yes it was!

A: How can it have been? I'm somewhere else!

Apart from these fantastic dialogues, traditional clowns also developed an amazing range of vocal games in their routines. For example: ridiculous tones of voice, use of rhythm and repetition, vocal sound effects (imitating animals, boats, ambulances, farts, etc.), onomatopoeias, elongating syllables or vowels within words, excessively emotional delivery and ridiculous ways of laughing or crying. This arsenal of vocal resources is still being used successfully in modern circus arenas by clowns who continue to update the traditional acts with inspirational wisdom.

It is also true that many clowns (both traditional and contemporary) have chosen not to use their voices on stage, and obviously they have the advantage of being able to work internationally without having to be multilinguists. The decision to use the voice or not when clowning is completely personal. Either you have a natural inclination to communicate through gestures and images, or, on the contrary, you have a natural talent with words (or sounds) and can use them to great comic effect. Clowns who are experts in quipping or word play would feel severely handicapped if they were unable to use this talent to get their laughs. Therefore, the decision to renounce or employ words should not depend on your ambition to perform world-wide. You should instead follow your internal instincts, which will tell you which choice will best allow your clown to reach his/her full expression.

As we've seen, becoming a great clown depends, to a large degree, on your ability to communicate with precision and clarity. Words are, evidently, first class tools for this task. But even a sound, used adequately, can add layers of meaning to your stage play. Your voice can, for example, highlight or explain an action, reinforce a physical gesture or change its significance completely. It can also amply express all the emotions and give away what you're really thinking.

There's so much to be gained from playing with one's voice and with words that I always recommend to my students that they conduct an extensive exploration of their vocal cords when they start out. Many of them need to be actively encouraged to use their voices in playful, weird or stupid ways, due to the fact that their vocal cords have had only one function for far too many years, that of reproducing words. Their voices have lost their creative capacities through simple neglect. Many students even find it difficult to get the words that are on the tip of their tongue out. Unfortunately, there exists a generalized tendency in adults toward self-censorship, and it's often so deeply ingrained that it's hard to overrule.

Be that as it may, I have witnessed a huge number of cases where students, through liberating their voices, have simultaneously released their clown from its hiding place. As they let the idiocies pour from their mouths, an irrepressible pleasure begins to well up and seize hold of them. This is due to the incredible power the voice exerts on human beings. Using our voices creatively, or listening to others doing so, releases our souls. We become joyful, light, emotional, centred or transported to other planes of consciousness. Thus, recovering your vocal freedom is a worthwhile endeavour. It is after all, one of our primal pleasures.

Oral experts

For the first eighteen months of our lives our oral sense is by far the most predominant. As babies, we spend our time gurgling, sucking and generally exploring the world through our mouths. But the oral experimentation doesn't end there. Inventing and playing with sounds and words is second nature throughout childhood; it's part of an essential learning process that leads to the accumulation of vocabulary and a proficiency in its use. Children assimilate the significance and usage of about 79,000 words between the ages of three and twelve. This process is no doubt driven by their desire to participate in conversations and have their needs met with greater ease. But it is under-pinned by their continuing fascination with the sensual pleasure of their vocal experimentations and the interesting effects the sounds they produce have on others. As a general rule, children aren't inclined to self constraint and this is particularly true with regards to their vocal chords; noises will slip out constantly!

Because their vocabulary is still very limited and their comprehension of the world even more so, children are waylaid by problems and errors when it comes to talking. But they seem undaunted by this. If they can't pronounce a letter (certain letters such as the r, the n, or the v require subtle and complicated coordination of the lips and tongue), they'll just bypass it; if they don't know the word for something, they'll invent one; if they don't understand everything that's being said, they'll extract whatever's comprehensible and reach conclusions based on their own logic; if a sound or word strikes them as funny, they'll repeat it endlessly, even at the risk of driving everyone else mad. Whatever strikes their fancy, whatever the occasion calls for, whatever seems right, they'll try it. Singing, for instance, is a frequent pleasure, and not necessarily limited to the mere repetition of known songs. They'll make up tunes and lyrics with surprising spontaneity. They'll also freely share with whoever's around every little detail of their lives; and even when on their own they don't stop talking; they'll have conversations with themselves or their toys or friendly imaginary beings.

Playing with the voice

Clearly, if you're still gathering effective tools for your clown, reopening an investigation into creative vocal gymnastics could prove extremely fruitful. I've found that beginners often reap their first real laughs when they're encouraged to add sound or words to their stage play. Those that have mistakenly sensed a yawning abyss between themselves and their audience find that their voices will bridge the gap far more easily than they suspected. So, if I see students having difficulties or looking creatively blocked, I'll ask them to vocalize the problem, or just say something without thinking about what, or make a sound; and as soon as they receive a positive response I'll get them to keep probing in that direction. Even just releasing one's breath can get a laugh.

As I have said, honesty and simplicity can both lead to laughter, but other games that I'll suggest are:

speak with the tongue out, emit strange sounds, imitate the sounds of emotionally charged animals (a happy pig, a mosquito in heat, etc.), mimic well known singers (of varying musical styles), explore possible rhythms (accelerating or de-celerating when speaking), increase or decrease the volume, play with the way to say a word, say something backwards, speak in an unknown language (or in a known one they aren't proficient in), make each sentence rhyme, speak as if reciting the classics.

The majority of these suggestions are easy to implement, but to become a skilled player requires practice. Personally, I think it's more interesting not to overload the action with an excess of unnecessary or pointless sound. Silence can be golden too, so do not be afraid to use it. As with physical action and emotional reactions, ideally everything spoken should lead to laughter or the enhancement of the comedy.

There are many ways to start training and playing again with your voice. You can take as a starting point any of the suggestions I've mentioned in this section, or of course you can invent your own. You can sing, babble, or gurgle in the shower, or while cooking, or even while listening to your favourite music. And, just in case you need further inspiration, here are some great word games that I've played with my family. We've laughed a lot playing them, and I hope you have an equal amount of fun with them. Invite your friends to join in!

- Maintain a conversation using known melodies, or songs or the anthem of your favourite football team.
- Change the lyrics or the emotional content of popular songs.
- Invent new words or names for everyday objects.
- Speak without using one, two or more letters of the alphabet.
- Talk for a minute on any topic that someone proposes without pauses, or hesitation or losing the thread of the argument.
- Always use the last word of the previous sentence to start a new sentence. Try to keep some logic in everything that you say.
- Talk in verse or in paired rhymes.
- Search for phrases from well-known songs that begin with each letter of the alphabet, from "A" onwards.

7
Succumb to temptation

There are many clown routines that have become "classics" over time but none more so than the one in which the Whiteface leaves a package, cake or an important object in the care of the Auguste. The Whiteface, before departing, always leaves strict instructions that under no circumstances should it be touched, much less opened, eaten or broken. But, almost as soon as he leaves, these instructions are blithely disobeyed. The Auguste, without an authority figure to persistently remind him of his responsibilities, is immediately plunged into a quandary of desire. The mere fact of having been forbidden to do something makes that very thing irresistible! Of course he heard the words "do not touch this" but, in his mind, this is not an unbreakable command; it's more like a stop line on the road: with a little vigilance it can be crossed. What possible harm could be done by just one itzy bitzy finger, one brief caress? And anyway, nobody will know! Well, certainly not the Whiteface, he's nowhere to be seen.

However, having once crossed the prohibiting line, the Auguste's insatiable curiosity always gets the better of him. Without thinking, he'll move closer to get a better look, then turn the thing around, shake it, smell it, taste it... until, of course, he ends up destroying or devouring it completely. So, when at last the Whiteface returns, the Auguste has no choice but to play the innocent. He'll try to convince the Whiteface that everything is as it was. When of course he inevitably fails to do so, he'll lay the blame on anyone handy before running as fast as he can towards the exit!

Such routines testify to the fact that succumbing to temptation is inevitable for red nosed clowns; it's part of their nature. They've never been mere observers of life and so consequently, they don't deny themselves the opportunities that arise to enjoy themselves. Their impulsive, sensual nature eggs them on, inciting them to go beyond what is permitted. And naturally, the audience wants them to go there, wants to see them flouting the rules and getting into trouble. With all this internal and external encouragement, temptations appear as if by magic and once perceived they're difficult, if not impossible, to resist.

The more fun you have, the more fun everyone will have

The above is a golden rule. So, just before heading out on stage to improvise, remind yourself what your real goal is: to have as much fun as possible!

My twenty-five plus years of experience have only helped confirm this fact; as a clown you have to take the plunge and start enjoying yourself just as soon as you can. You've got to let your imagination fly, listen to your heart's desires, speak your mind, move as you please, be emotionally generous; in short, be fully alive, regardless of the consequences. You have to make a conscious choice; to act on that insistent inner voice that urges you towards freedom. Obviously, when you give yourself permission to go further than you would normally go (to exaggerate, reveal and experiment more), the risk you take is that of finding yourself at some point in a sticky situation: getting into trouble, clashing with authority, etc. But don't let that deter you! If you don't take risks and follow your own inner promptings, you'll never find out that all these situations are in fact gifts. Clowns thrive on them, for it's then that they have to be at their most ingenious.

Transgression

Clowning comes with a price. You have to accept that some people will disapprove of your decision to clown around. They may be strangers, or acquaintances, or even friends and family, but at some point or other you'll encounter someone who doesn't understand your vital drive.

Before sending students out on the street to clown here in Spain, I warn them that it will be the pensioners, immigrants and children who'll most likely appreciate their efforts. This may be because they have fewer prejudices; or because they come from cultures where spontaneous communication with strangers is more common; or because they share with clowns something of their marginal status: they know what it is to live on the threshold of society rather than at its centre. I also warn them that they'll receive positive reactions from people, but that there'll be other types of reactions too; indifferent, negative and, exceptionally, violent. The red nose in an urban space produces conflicting emotions; those who wear one are abnormal and are therefore unpredictable: a cause for concern for certain people.

It may sometimes seem, that in putting on a red nose, you are swimming against the tide, but you're not. Increasingly I find myself welcoming students from all walks of life: doctors, psychologists, gardeners, journalists, teachers, carpenters, social workers, policemen, politicians, entrepreneurs, bakers, firefighters, yoga teachers, etc. There's evidence, therefore, to suggest that Western society is undergoing an important shift, as more and more people are willing to jump overboard and abandon the ship of respectability. People who are not only wanting to laugh at themselves and their constraints but moreover, wanting to do it publicly.

> "It's not a sign of health to be well adapted to a sick society."
> *Jiddu Krishnamurti, spiritual philosopher, India*

Clowns have traditionally been seen as a marginal group of individuals who don't fit the system's profile of "a productive person". They're clearly impervious to consumerist values, ignorant of etiquette, and form no part of the moral majority. In the eyes of society, they have nothing; neither power, nor beauty, nor money; nor even normal brain cells! They belong with the wretched poor.

Be that as it may, clowns assume this role with ease; they have their own scale of values and a perspective on reality tinged with humour. And it's precisely this indestructible sense of humour, in the face of the misfortunes and complications of life, that calls into question who the really wretched are. Aren't those who suffer from stress, bad-tempered moodiness and almost continuous dissatisfaction the truly wretched? Are not those who seldom pay attention to their deepest desires the unfortunate ones?

> "We don't become adults, we become adulterated."
> *Tortell Poltrona, clown, Spain*

Clowns are the descendants of court jesters, commedia dell'arte players, and the ambulant theatrical comedians of the 16th century. Their ancestors were anarchic nonconformists who habitually poked fun at the authorities, questioned the reigning morality and openly criticized the rulers and their laws. They were transgressors in every sense of the word; their actions, declarations and emotional outbursts habitually crossed every regulatory line. They gave themselves the license to be free, and in doing so, they challenged those who wished to keep the masses enslaved.

Contemporary clowns continue to pay homage to their inheritance, following in the footsteps of their ancestors by breaching social and theatrical conventions. Individual clowns will misbehave to a greater or lesser extent. Some will go much further than others, but all cross, at some point or other, those invisible lines that normally hold us back. Clowns transgress on various fronts: by showing themselves for who they really are, by sharing openly how they feel and think, by always allowing a margin for improvisation in their performances, by playing with taboo subjects (death, sex, violence, etc.), and by ignoring the established social (and sometimes legal) boundaries. They even transgress the universal laws of logic and physics, showing how the impossible can be made possible; arms or legs stretching till they're six feet long, bodies suddenly able to fly, hair that can revolve on heads like helicopter propellers, shoes with mouths that move, umbrellas that pour rain, indoor snow storms out of nowhere, etc.

When you put on a red nose, you will suddenly find that you have been given a license to freedom. You'll find you're able to: take more liberties with people, follow your subconscious urges, break through limitations, interpret events and situations in your own way, refrain from deciding in advance how you're going to feel, choose not to accept "no" for an answer, gain first hand experience, expound your thoughts, refuse to take things at face value, and share what is most important to you. Your clown has, miraculously, managed to avoid the conditioning process that turns us into responsible adults. As a clown you will never be in danger of getting bored, because the world around you becomes a giant game board, with a host of new experiences yet to be lived.

Constant research

To help my students rediscover the wonders of the world that surrounds them, I send them out on the street in small groups with the following instructions:

"You have just arrived from another planet. You don't speak or understand the language, nor do you have any information about the species here and their customs. You have been sent on a mission to discover all you can about these things, to explore this world they call "Earth" and report back in thirty minutes."

After a mere half an hour they return, their faces glowing with the surprise of having encountered so many fascinating things:

I couldn't help just staring at the sky the whole time. There were so many different colours to define! Then I noticed these whitish, greyish blobs that moved very slowly up there. I thought maybe these were a type of earthly transportation system. A winged species flew by overhead, it was so graceful I tried to imitate it.

I saw an old man sitting on a bench. As the two were immobile, I assumed that they were one inanimate unified thing. I moved to observe this "thing" from a different angle and noticed that its eyes followed me. I imitated the eye movement and the thing's lips smiled at me. I copied the gesture trying to understand its meaning. Its hand moved to scratch its face, I imitated that too. This was a strange species! Gradually, it began to play with me. Knowing that I would mimic its gestures, it began to make more and more ridiculous ones.

I was immersed in watching a very small species crawl across the palm of my hand when a couple of humans approached me. They were curious about what I had seen that was so very interesting.

Before temptation can beckon you, something or someone must first capture your attention with enough force to make you feel drawn towards them. But, as a clown, you don't have to witness a miracle in order for this to happen. The "something" you see that ignites your interest can be a mundane object and the "someone" simply the first person you set your eyes on when you walk out onstage. The truth is that with a simple change in your normal perspective, anything or anyone can captivate you instantly. Jump-starting your interest works like this: you decide to forget what you know about the world and suddenly you'll find yourself being curious about everything again.

"The clown creates a world in an empty space, instead of entering a world that already exists."
Avner The Eccentric, clown, U.S.A.

Training yourself to remain curious about the world around you and those who populate it will definitely help you in your clowning. Many clown exercises offer only very open-ended instructions; in reality you can take them in any direction you feel like. You come out from behind the screen or curtain on to a bare stage, or at most, one with a solitary chair, and, "hey presto! just start playing!" If, right then, the eternal question "what am I supposed to do?" pops into your mind, it will probably be because you have forgotten to focus your attention on the details around you. I've seen students creating wonderful games out of the most unexpected things, simply because they became interested enough in them. The bits of tape on the stage floor, the shadows on the back wall, the creak of a floor board, the blinding brightness of a spotlight, the gaping space at the end of the stage, a radiator on the wall, a ball of fluff on a jumper, a nail protruding from a wall, a thread hanging from a sleeve, a person in the audience coughing, the specks of dust in the air; all have been the beginnings of hilarious clown improvisations.

Infant curiosity

Human beings, throughout history, have been obsessed by the desire to know more; to understand the why's and wherefore's of life. Being inquisitive is actually your natural state of being. All young children possess an incurable curiosity. Adult theories, about how things are or the way things work, don't hold much sway over them. They're willing to learn or unlearn something, but only through practical experiments. Try telling them that they shouldn't climb up to dangerous heights or eat any old thing they find on the floor. Until they fall off the back of a chair or taste something really revolting, they'll not show much sign of having understood your words. Through their delighted wonder about life, they remind us that curiosity is synonymous with vitality. Without wonder we cease to flourish as human beings.

Knowing the principal components of childhood inquisitiveness could prove to be very useful when you forget to ignore everything you know when clowning. So here's a brief survey of them:

1. Making sense of things

Children are constantly facing new situations. Sometimes these situations can prove pleasurable, but actually, the vast majority are more likely to be strange or complicated, resulting in feelings of confusion, uncertainty or stress. However, being accustomed to not understanding immediately the things they encounter, children are prepared to wait for clarification; they'll observe, try practical experiments and absorb the information presented to them *before* reaching conclusions. Their primary intention is understanding how things work. What's the meaning of an action, reaction or word? Why do things happen the way they do? What uses do different objects have? Why do things make sounds? How can you tell that you're hungry?

As their knowledge is still so very limited they will often reach mistaken conclusions. Vidal Pérez, a student, told me these stories from his childhood:

> *I remember being convinced that my father controlled the traffic lights using the gear stick of our car, because every time that the lights changed to green he was shifting gear. Another memory I have is of my mother returning home several times saying miserably, "They didn't give me the meat" — or so I thought. She was actually saying they wouldn't give*

her a driving license (in Spanish, the word for license is "carné" which sounds very like "carne", the word for meat). As she failed the test repeatedly, (seventeen times!), I became convinced that the butcher was a brute who sometimes refused to deal with her, and since it seemed to make her so unhappy, I couldn't understand why she didn't simply go to a different butcher's shop!

If children do not find a rational explanation for events there is always the magical option. They believe in magic and in magical beings; both are very real and active in their world. Another of Vidal's memories:

When I was small I believed that tennis players were magicians. I never noticed that there were boys who passed them the balls. I thought the players made them appear out of nowhere; they amazed me.

2. Asking for asking's sake
Anyone who has spent time with children knows that they ask a lot of questions. At times, they can be incredibly persistent, firing out question after question, seemingly obsessed with getting the answers to life's big questions. It's blatantly obvious though, that during these "interrogation sessions", knowing the answer to their questions isn't that important to them. They've an ulterior motive for their endless probing: pleasure. They simply adore thinking up another question,

playing the game of asking about things. Where did the first fork come from? Why do people sleep? Who invented rice pudding? What makes me grow?

With my daughter Amara, for a fair number of years, these quiz hours were a real challenge to my quick-wittedness. Responding correctly more often than not proved impossible without resorting to a virtual encyclopedia on the sly. She would invent question after question after question, until I'd put a stop to it. In the end her questioning became such a joking point that, before she'd start a session of questions, she'd ask me: "Mum, can I ask, just for asking's sake, if I could ask a question or two?"

3. What will happen if... ?

What will happen if I... put water in my pocket... throw my toys onto the street from the balcony... do a belly operation on my favourite stuffed animal... squash my food on grandpa's head... paint my father's suits?

Infants, from the time they begin to crawl, will actively explore their environment at every opportunity. When something catches their eye, they'll go and investigate, and if during that investigation they find an entertaining game, so much the better. They can happily spend ten to fifteen minutes with a few cooking pots and a wooden spoon, discovering the principles of cause and effect, volume and weight, tactility and musicality. It goes without saying that they pick up an amazing amount of useful knowledge through play, but let's not forget that they also create some impressive messes! Furthermore, they will get themselves into some very tricky situations, for example: becoming hopelessly entangled in their clothing because of wanting to try it on the wrong way round, climbing up a tree with the agility of a goat only to realise they don't know how to get back down again, pulling on the tablecloth and bringing down a table full of crockery on their heads because they wanted to use the cloth as a blanket for their doll, emptying a full bottle of shampoo in the bath because they wanted to see what was in the very bottom of the bottle, cutting a large chunk of hair from their heads just to see if it would hurt.

Children are pint-sized scientists researching the world through an endless set of experiments. They delight in making new discoveries and love sharing them with others. Their findings are duly stored in their brains, to be applied when seemingly similar situations arise. But it goes without saying that they often get it wrong, and simply find themselves in another messy predicament!

Messing around

When my daughter was ten years old I wrote the following in my diary:

> *Amara still gets distracted from the work in hand or the job to be done, as easily as a five year old. It's different now though: before it was play and now it's her fantasy world that enthralls her. It's her mind that loses concentration on the task she's been told to*

do (brush your teeth, put your pyjamas on, lay the table, etc.). She'll easily get a crazy flash when there is something "adult" to do. I suppose it's just a drag for her to have to do things that she doesn't want to, so her mind wanders into greener pastures. Suddenly she loses track of the action in progress, her eyes take on a faraway look and then she's off and away either dancing in the living room still dripping wet from the bath, or snipping away at magazines with the nail clipper... I'm loathe to tell her to stop messing around as if messing around were something bad or not good for her — so instead I use a line from a wonderful Michael Rosen poem called Bathroom Dillydallying.

The poem describes, from a child's perspective, the adventures to be had in a bathroom with the toothpaste, talcum powder and soap suds. At the end of the poem the child simply gets lost in the experience of sucking on a sponge, the word "sponge" expanding in his brain, echoing back on itself again and again.

So now when Amara flies away with Peter Pan I remind her that time is a factor that can't always be ignored — especially at the end of the day — I say "Amara, you're sucking on a sponge again." Because she knows the poem, she smiles, drawn back to her parents' world. In this way we laugh about her wanderings, recognise them not only as normal child behaviour but also as a very worthwhile occupation; essential, in fact, when creating in any art form.

Clowns mess around; they'll do and say ridiculous things and their shows are full of foolishness. Wonderful foolishness that sometimes borders on pure genius, sometimes on sub-lime stupidity. Yes, messing around means doing something idiotic, like trying to act out Hamlet without even having read the play, or performing a feat of magic and then revealing the trick you used. Or when someone calls you on stage saying, "Come here now", you go up to them and ask, "What, here? Now?" and when the other nods, you reply, "Okay, I'll come here now", and then disappear only to nonchalantly return three seconds later. It's idiotic to put a plastic tap on your forehead, turn it, and spurt a jet of water from your mouth; stupid to put on clothes that are far too tight for you so that as soon as you bend over they rip along the seams; stupid to climb up a ladder and then remember you've a fear of heights.

Yes, clowns do and say many foolish things. But that is just an indication of their wisdom. They have four very good reasons for engaging in foolishness:

1. "A fool thinks himself to be wise, but a wise man knows himself to be a fool."
William Shakespeare

These days we're all under a constant pressure to be clever (or at least pretend to be); but try-ing to be smart all the time limits our creativity immensely. When clowning, if you're attempting to be smart, to find that great idea that puts your intelligence in the limelight and makes you look good in front of others, you'll discard many "stu-pid" ideas, ideas that will actually be far funnier than the clever quips you're desperately trying to find. You'll also miss out on all the opportunities to succumb to temptation, because you'll be in your head rather than with your senses.

Professional clowns aren't concerned about looking smart, but that is not to say they reject their own intelligence. They may do lots of crazy things, but don't let that dupe you — messing around requires an enormous amount of mental agility. Through not attempting to prove how intelligent they are, they can access an even deeper intelligence, freely associating ideas, sometimes in rapid succession, surprising even themselves with their ingenuity. These moments of unfettered creativity are extremely liberating for the brain and the resulting experience is pure pleasure.

2. "Only two things are infinite, the universe and human stupidity. And I'm not sure about the former."
Albert Einstein

As I explained in chapter 4, clowns put human beings under a comic magnifying glass. But even without that magnifying glass it is plain to see that humans do stupid things. We are the most intelligent species on our planet and our evolution has been spectacular. In just two thousand years we have practically monopolized the whole of the planet; we've built up civilizations, eradicated many threats to our survival, invented a myriad of objects to facilitate our existence. We have also created a cultural heritage, dominated natural resources, explored space, etc. But, even so, we have never ceased to be stupid.

One could argue that we spend most of our lives doing nonsensical things without ever being fully aware of it. When we're young we want to be old and when we're old, young again. We deny the existence of death whilst running towards it. We fill our world with poisonous products and then worry about our health and safety. We look for happiness in disposable gadgets. We always want to be right even when we know we're not. We value our bank account more than nature. We fall madly in love with someone and shortly thereafter we hate that same person whole-heartedly. And the most conclusive evidence of all: our unshakeable belief in our own superior importance.

In this infinite universe, our tiny galaxy, the Milky Way, is composed of a mere 100,000 million to 200,000 million stars, while some of the larger ones encompass over a trillion stars. In addition, our particular Solar system is 30,000 light years from the centre of our galaxy. The Earth is not even the most important star in the Solar system, the Sun is over a million times bigger. Seen from this perspective, you and I are no big or important thing. To think that our intelligence is supreme is really a monumental stupidity.

3. "Most researchers would agree that humour involves an idea, image, text, or event that is somewhat incongruous, weird, unusual, surprising or out of the ordinary. In addition, there must be some aspect that makes us evaluate the stimulus as not serious or minor, putting us in a playful state of mind, at least momentarily".

This summary is from *The Psychology of Humour, an Integrative Approach*, by Rod A. Martin, a psychology professor, who includes in his book a forty-eight page reference section. I doubt that any empirical study (since 1950) on any aspect of humour has been overlooked, so it's fair to say that this fully informed academic knows what he's talking about.

It could be said then that the essential ingredients for provoking laughter are: incongruity, surprise and playfulness. Consequently it's clear that doing something normal or obvious isn't going to get you a laugh. There has to be an element, in what the audience sees you doing, that shifts their frame of reference. If they know that your actions are not to be taken seriously they're more likely to want to take part in the game. At the same time they have to perceive a discrepancy: that something is not as it should be, that there's a contradiction, or that you're not using normal logic. And finally, they have to be surprised, not with just anything, but with something that ensues from what's already happened, something new that has some connection with preceding events. If this connection is lacking, instead of laughing, they'll be puzzled. So, what could be a better way to meet these three requirements than to mess around?

4. "Fantasy is what puts in place the foundations of our ability to create, imagine, think and project. Fantasy frees us from the mundane, taking us beyond the obvious, the superficial, the plain

reality of the present. It's a capacity without which humans would not be as we are."
Luciano Montero, excerpt from *The Adventure of Growing Up (La Aventura de Crecer)*.

If messing around releases our spontaneity, stimulates our creativity, improves our sense of humour and frees us from mental blockages, naturally it's also going to encourage us to fantasize. Fooling around will fan the flames of your imagination, presenting you with the ideas that create original or wacky situations on stage.

In theatres and circuses fantastical things can and should happen. Both are, after all, illusory worlds, filled with fictional characters. During a brief period of time, the spectators can be transported to an alternative reality; somewhere strangely familiar or spectacularly unknown. Contemporary clowns, even though they're not always found in circus arenas or on theatrical stages, still have their roots in these fanciful places, where nothing was what it seemed to be. It's hardly surprising then, that clowns' imaginations became very active; that their shows incorporated ever more wacky props, innovative ideas and surprising costumes.

What would human life be like without such foolishness? Without leaps of imagination? Without the fearless few prepared to risk being seen as nonsensical? Throughout history, many ideas (such as: the Earth is a round sphere which revolves around the Sun) were scorned and ridiculed by the "knowledgeable", who claimed they were absolute nonsense. Some of these ideas proved visionary, springing from the minds of truly illuminated beings. Leonardo da Vinci, considered the most versatile genius of all time, wrote: "Our greatest stupidities may in fact be very wise". Five hundred years on and we're still having to vindicate the incredible value of our idiotic ideas and actions!

A sense of humour

Last in this chapter, but not by any means the least important: you have to succumb to all the above temptations in the funniest way possible, you have to apply a sense of humour to every situation you encounter. However, even though almost everyone agrees that having a sense of humour is something desirable, even valuable, what is our definition of a sense of humour? Do we all have the same one?

To find out, I interviewed a group of students, and their answers to this were very varied:

> *It's first knowing how to laugh about yourself, your body, the things that happen to you, etc., and then joking about others.*

> *It's not having prejudices, being authentic and having a philosophy of acceptance towards life.*

> *It's being able to distance oneself a bit from reality in order to see life from a different viewpoint. A sense of humour helps you step outside a situation for a moment, and realise the absurdity of it or the funny side of it, and that's very healthy.*

> *It is the ability to see the double meaning in a sentence and to have a pressure relief valve when you*

interact with others. It has saved me from some very
embarrassing situations.

These responses indicate that a sense of humour is something very personal, which is to say, it's relative and subjective. These four opinions suggest that a sense of humour can mean: the capacity to laugh out loud, an open and positive outlook on life, a device that alters reality, a means of overcoming adversity, a cognitive exercise that promotes health, a way of showing intelligence, a social skill that relieves interpersonal tensions, and a self-defence mechanism. I would add to this list: an expression that makes us feel exuberant and, of course, the ability to provoke laughter in others.

Clowns are in the humour business. For many, a clown is simply "someone who makes people laugh". In my opinion, it's essential to meet this widespread expectation, although there are clowns (especially those of the Russian school) who don't believe that it's so important. Making people laugh, or stimulating other people's sense of humour, is not an easy task, but neither is it mission impossible. Throughout this book I explain the ABC's of the techniques used by clowns to achieve this goal: authenticity, failure, foolishness, playfulness, exaggeration, surprise, etc. Individually these can be very effective, and as a whole, a comic bombshell! Obviously you have to personalize and integrate each of these concepts, and make them work for you on stage. Your interpretation of the techniques however, will depend mostly on your sense of humour, and on how you use and habitually express it.

I can immediately identify students who regularly make other people laugh. Their sense of humour is honed and natural but they're not necessarily extroverts. They're aware of the talent they possess and so they're relaxed. Their sense of humour supports and guides them, and gives them the necessary confidence to be comfortable on stage. They know that they can count on it to get them out of any sticky situation, and so they take greater risks and enjoy themselves more than those less given to finding life humorous.

In the first workshops that I gave in Peru (2009), I had the pleasure of working with two groups of students who all had an excellent sense of humour. Franco Cabrera was one of them. He never did anything in a straightforward manner, always surprising his audience with his comic twists and turns. In one improvisation (exercise 4, chapter 9) Franco, facing the back wall with his eyes closed, announced:

I am going to turn 180° to the North, positioning myself perpendicularly to the audience. I am then going to open my eyes as wide as possible and move towards my partner as if I had reggae music riffs running around in my head.

With the first sentence he already had us laughing; his remark was so scrupulously precise it was ridiculous. Anticipating his actions, we continued laughing, eager to see how he'd execute what he'd stated. The visual images his body made didn't disappoint us. He was tall and thin, and his initial precision followed by his undulating movements, were a delight to watch. Franco could reap hilarity from everything he did or said, so much so that he could repeat a phrase or action as many times as he wanted to, and still get us to laugh enthusiastically.

If you're like Franco, you only need to let yourself flow and you'll find the comedy. But if you're not, don't worry, because your ability to make people laugh, even when unused, never dies completely. A sense of humour is like a muscle, the more you use it, the stronger it becomes. You just need to start cultivating it, day by day.

Before launching into your daily practice, it's important to recognise that you actually like making people laugh (whether it's just your intimate circle of family and friends or a wider public), and that you are able to do so (even if it's just one person at a time). Personally, when someone else makes me laugh my enjoyment is different from when I make others laugh. When I succeed in generating laughter, I'm gratified. And to my knowledge, there isn't a person alive who doesn't feel that same pleasure and satisfaction (openly or secretly), in being the exponent and instigator of the happiness laughter expresses.

There are two ways to create humour: the premeditated and the spontaneous. Jokes, gags, funny anecdotes, word play, irony and pranks fall into the first category. In the second; spontaneous witticisms or physical antics, peculiar or eccentric behaviour, minor accidents and gaffes. Most of the humour that we experience day to day belongs to this second category. It happens without premeditation, in the course of our social relations. Most of the time we can easily fail to notice that we're either practicing or participating in the art of being funny, unless of course, the laughter that's provoked is so loud or prolonged that it becomes obvious.

Those whose profession is clowning however, are well aware of this type of humour. Even amusing nuances will not go unnoticed by them, as they could be a future source of inspiration. All the professional clowns with whom I've spoken, enthusiastically observed the comedy in their own lives and willingly recounted personal anecdotes about their misfortunes and fortunes with a lively sense of humour.

Paloma Reyes, a Brazilian clown, explained her sense of humour this way:

I'm always looking for ways to make myself laugh, and practise my sense of humour every day. And yes, on stage I'm conscious of the comic resources I have to make others laugh, and these resources I sift from my life experiences. I use them because what happens to my clown on the stage also happens to me in real life. I always see the ridiculous side of all that happens to me, humour rescues me when I hit rock bottom. I see things from the outside and I think, 'Ah, this could be very funny!' It may be that something really serious is happening to me, but with a little effort, seeing things through the eyes of my clown, I see the other side, their funny side.

So you don't have to have a talent for wise-cracking, or know a lot of good jokes, or be capable of regularly delivering great punch lines to be a clown (although if you have these skills they will undoubtedly prove useful). But you do have to start consciously registering the comedy that surrounds you.

"You only have to look around and you will find there's humor everywhere."
Mr Di, clown, Spain

To help with the task, here's a recap of some of the pointers mentioned in this chapter:
- Remain alert and curious.
- Admit your own ridiculousness.
- Use your intelligence; your emotional, corporeal and interpersonal intelligence.
- Look for the funny, ironic, absurd, incoherent, ridiculous or stupid in all that happens.
- Share your discoveries with others.

Everyone has their own sense of humour and it is important to start from there. What do you find funny? How do you make other people laugh? When do you laugh and with whom? As you expand your awareness of the things, people or places that put you in a good mood, you'll also begin to perceive how you can shift into good humour and participate in creating it more actively.

When it comes down to it, we all find human imperfection funny. We are only human, we have many faults, and when someone recognises their own with humour, we love them for it. If they then point out other human foibles, we'll join them in laughing at ourselves.

The clown shouts from the stage, "Would like to see this?" and his audience shouts back, "Yes!"
He eggs them on, "Louder, please! Do you want to see this?"
"Yes!" they shout back even more enthusiastically.
"Why?" he fires out quickly.
"Yes!" they all shout in unison, unable to change the momentum.
The clown freezes on the spot, "Yes? Why yes? Ha, normally when I ask why, they can't tell me. In Germany, in answer to my 'why?' there's silence. In France I ask why? — nothing. But in Spain, when I say 'why?' you all answer, 'Yes!' Interesting."

8
The loser's corner

Everyone knows that clowns make people laugh with their crazy antics and over-the-top foolery, but what many people don't know is a large part of their job description requires them almost continually to encounter and battle with failure. And what's more, they have to acknowledge their failures publicly! An ordinary person would shy away from such a challenge and if forced into it would probably sink rather than swim. By contrast, clowns use every flop to their advantage — in fact, being a loser actually guarantees their professional success.

In the clown classroom, I have found that the more time I spend on the theme of failure with beginners, the quicker they discover important aspects of their clown. By preventing them from achieving the things I ask of them, by giving them incentives to make mistakes or put their foot in it, and by insisting that they don't have to be competitive or defensive, I am actually helping them to move forward with greater ease. My intention is that they experience first hand how differently these moments of difficulty feel when they adopt the clown's philosophy (so radically different from their own) and allow themselves to be ridiculous. The results are both funny and moving.

Resetting the way to look upon and live failure has become an indispensable part of my methodology, not only because it's fundamental to successful clowning, but also because the clown's way of tackling life's knocks and bumps can also be applied to real life difficulties.

On the battlefield

Among the first games that I get my beginner students to play, is a game I call 'The Sword'. Its goal is to get students to start admitting their mistakes publicly while still enjoying themselves. I ask them to stand in a circle and then explain that they have to jump, duck, or move backwards to avoid being killed by an imaginary sword I will wield in all directions. If they don't get it right — for example, if they crouch when they should have jumped, or if they don't react fast enough to prevent a fatal blow — they must melodramatically ham up their deaths, before falling dead on the floor. Those left standing are then asked to applaud and praise the dead, thanking them for their honest acknowledgement of their failure.

Very often the first time this game is played the participants are extremely reluctant to admit that they didn't react correctly. One person, at the most, may fall to the ground, and usually because I've looked at them quizzically or made it clear that I did in fact see them getting their heads or legs chopped off. However, a day later I repeat the game and the scene is completely different: it's a battlefield! There's imaginary blood spouting all over the place, and everyone's dying in the most bizarre ways. Often I'm the only person left standing because they've all realised that it's much more fun to die spectacularly and receive a round of applause than be the one who just stands there and claps. So even those who have successfully evaded the sword have still dramatically dropped to the floor. How do I achieve this? By working on accepting and expressing vulnerability.

The magic moment

I begin working on this by telling students, "I'm now going to ask the impossible of you. On stage, as clowns, I'm going to put you in situations that make success unachievable." I warn them beforehand so that they understand, at least on an intellectual level, that my objective will be to make them fail, but that it's the clown I want to see failing, not them as people, so they should not take my instructions or comments personally.

To get the ball rolling I propose an exercise in which they have to present a children's story (with all the characters, dialogues and scenes) but then deliberately give them only a minute in which to complete the representation. They get to do this in pairs, but even so, performing The Three Little Pigs for example, in just sixty seconds is creatively challenging. Most people have been overly educated in doing things "correctly", so they'll automatically throw themselves into completing the task as well as possible. They'll go back stage and I'll hear them trying to plan something in order to avoid a fiasco, even though this means losing valuable time and thus making their task even more difficult.

Obviously, what they still have not grasped is that assigning roles in advance will make certain hilarious clowning moments impossible; for instance when two clowns enter playing the wolf and then spend the rest of the time fighting over who's better suited for the role, or when one of the clowns plays all the characters while the other tries unsuccessfully to butt in before resigning herself to becoming a tree.

Instead of these crazy situations, the duos attempt to give a straight rendering of the original story, most of the time completely ignoring the audience and the job of making people laugh. Their overzealous desire to reach the happy ending and thus complete the task correctly, makes them lose sight of all the fun they can have along the way. Even if I tell them that among the hundreds of clown students who have done this exercise only one pair managed to reach the end of the story, they still can't help trying to be the second!

Naturally, I also explain that no-one, from the age of five onwards, wants to see a straightforward, boringly faithful representation of Sleeping Beauty. We want surprises; we want the prince to have an aversion to kissing, or the mirror to forget its lines or proclaim the evil queen's dog the prettiest of them all, or we want the dwarfs to be unable to stop singing "Hi ho!" even when Snow White dies. In short, we want a twist to the tale, we want things to go wrong. But hearing my words is one thing, acting upon them quite another.

When the allotted time is over I blow a whistle, a sound that signals universally the end of striving, that the game is over, definitively. When they hear it something wonderful happens, for in that moment the stress of having to meet deadlines and expectations just falls away, and with it, all the social masks and physical tensions. Fragile, bereft of excuses or defences, only half way through their task (or still on the first scene), they surrender with a long exhalation, their faces a picture of human failure. This raw acceptance of defeat is so powerfully comical that those watching are moved to laughter. For a magical instant they see their own reflection, their own tragi-comic existence played out by the clowns.

Typically, the students on stage don't feel the comedy of the situation. Almost immediately their defences reappear, they play down their disappointment, diminish the importance of their failure and stop feeling vulnerable. They know that the next thing required is to look at their audience and show them what they feel about what they've done, but because they've buried what they really feel, most of them just look blank. However, everyone, audience and clowns alike, have become aware of that moment of human vulnerability and witnessed how it can, not only make us laugh, but also open up our hearts.

Our right to be vulnerable

Obviously, we all have a natural resistance to acknowledging our faults and failures. In childhood we felt marked by them, they were outright tragedies. Certainly, "they're going to laugh at me over this" doesn't sound like much fun when you're young. It is, however, purely a matter of education. I have found that children will openly and freely admit that they've made a mistake or failed in some way, if they know they'll not be made to feel guilty, be blamed or punished for it. When my daughter was four years old she accidentally dropped a plate of food on the floor, as I approached she blurted out: "Oops! I dropped it, but everyone drops things, don't they? — like everyone drop things in the toilet."

Both in my courses and in the world of clowning the norms on correct behaviour are turned on their head. Students suddenly find themselves in a place where they have to fail and celebrate their faults and shortcomings. Stupidity and ridiculousness, normally so derided, become valuable attributes that gain them approval and recognition. "You were so stupid" is an accolade, and "What a disaster!" a compliment. With this kind of encouragement I soon see my students relaxing, lowering their defences and become much more willing to take risks. Once the pressure of competing to be the best is removed, people will surprise you; they'll even surprise themselves, discovering latent talents and hidden resilience.

It goes without saying that nobody is as perfect as they'd like to be. However, in our highly competitive society it's becoming more and more difficult to admit that things are not going as well as we would like them to. We somehow feel we have to pretend, at least in certain social encounters, that we are quite capable of dealing with adversity, and that we and our lives are perfect. What great pains we take to cover up the truth! The truth being that almost every day we face problems of differing proportions, normally of our own making — we misplace the car keys, lose our way, break something valuable, get our heart broken, pretend we know something when we don't, bang, hit or hurt ourselves physically, forget something important, botch the job, say something stupid, etc. In other words, we're imperfect people and we lead imperfect lives.

Recently, however, the idea that failing is not such a bad thing has gradually begun to filter into certain sectors of our society. In many innovative business projects, failing is now considered more of a necessary building block than a stumbling block. Many people are thus promoting the benefits that can be reaped by reacting differently to our failures. The acceptance of personal error has come to be seen as a first step on the path to deeper understanding, renewed creativity and greater success. People are asking themselves, "What I can learn from this situation?" Within the personal growth world I've also repeatedly heard the phrase, "Everything is always perfect." The conclusion in all the above cases is that lingering in negative states is neither healthy nor necessary. Instead we should look directly for the positive in all situations.

Personally, I am not against suffering less, transforming painful experiences through stepping back and learning from them or having a positive attitude in the face of difficulty. I also firmly believe that everything that happens in the physical realm can aid our soul's journey. But, if we always leap into a positive stance automatically, in denial of what we are actually feeling, we lose sight of our vulnerability; we fail to acknowledge the fragility of our existence, our life, our world. Systematically overlooking this fragility has very serious side effects, in fact it's causing disasters on a global scale. But most of us still find it much more reassuring to keep the blindfold on. Being vulnerable has far too many negative (and painful) associations. If we allow ourselves to be vulnerable aren't we're giving in to weakness and opening ourselves up for attack?

Clowns, in that magic instant of surrender, are actually only being honest. They're showing that things affect them, that they have to suddenly modify their expectations of a desired outcome, do some internal adjusting, pause. But this doesn't change what they know or how they feel about themselves. Clowns have already accepted the fact that they are not the cleverest, bravest, or strongest people in the world, and that neither are they the most handsome, important, or talented. They have no pretensions, no perfect identity to defend, so it's easy for them to acknowledge their mistakes, live their vulnerability, and then play with both. Clowns freely explore their constant encounters with the problems of existence *before* moving on. And yes, they'll always bounce back and move on with a positive attitude, until, of course, the next pratfall!

Pamela

Pamela came to one of the advanced courses I taught with Alex Navarro in Peru. Her clown was full of life, explosive and hilarious. When she entered the stage she seemed to just let rip, let her sense of humour lead the way, confident that it would take her where she needed to go. Neither she, nor we, ever knew what was going to happen next, but nobody doubted that it would be entertaining. In her first individual improvisations she left her classmates marveling in admiration of her talent.

On the surface then, she seemed to have absolutely no qualms about baring herself completely, she looked fearless. But there were a number of tell-tale signs that told a different story. Her blind allegiance to her own madness bordered on the reckless, and sometimes she went too far. She offended or physically hurt her fellow clowns; she hogged the focus, passing it to the others with great reluctance (at our insistence) only to grab it again the instant she felt the energy dropping even half a degree; and her attitude to the audience at times felt unpleasant, as if she didn't care what we thought or felt about her actions. My impression of her was that of a competitive surfer: her ambition was to ride the crest of a comic wave, and stay there at all costs, regardless of the consequences.

Pamela was unable to take a breather or be still because, as she freely admitted, those empty spaces made her nervous. In fact the sensations of being defenceless, disarmed or vulnerable induced such panic in her that she just steamrollered right over them. Unfortunately, that meant that nothing could affect her and her clown lacked a heart. I therefore proposed that she tried taking short breaks when performing, in order to begin to feel more comfortable within the pauses. Unsurprisingly, she was more than willing to try, but admitted to feeling discomfort every time she allowed us to see her gentler side. We, however, saw how much beauty she radiated when she was soft and receptive and encouraged her to keep letting herself rest.

Pamela struggled creatively with her fears in every performance she gave. One of her improvisations played out in the following manner:

She squeezes her hands through the gap between the two screens we have placed side by side at the back of the stage. Her fingers explore the gap sliding upwards and downwards before returning to the centre, they then grapple with the screens, pushing them slowly apart by about three centimeters. Her fingers disappear slowly, now all we can see are her lips, pursed in an effort to reach through the gap. "I'm not going to do anything at all!" she says with difficulty because she's still keeping her lips pursed. She pauses while we laugh. "No, really, don't expect anything because you'll only be disappointed, I'm not going to do anything, no, nothing at all." She pauses again and there's more laughter. Her lips disappear only to be replaced by her left eye, checking out our reaction. We laugh again as one of her fingers re-appears and begins to gesticulate: 'no, nothing's going to happen, I'm not coming out from behind here.'

Her eye scrunches up, studying us; we are still laughing. Her finger suddenly hooks on to a screen and pulls it further apart. Her entire face squeezes through. "That's all there is folks," she says, "in fact I'm doing too much already. Less, I have to do less!" She frantically tries to pull the screens together but does not remove her face, so it ends up hopelessly squashed between the two. The image is so ridiculous we laugh again.

"Less. I have to do less." Her jaw is hardly able to move, so the words are slightly strangled. "Just the mouth. I've only got to show my mouth." She slides her forehead backwards, but the screens fall together unexpectedly, trapping her clown nose.

"Oh, no!" she intones in a tiny voice, "somebody...
help me!" We laugh but no one steps forward. She
waits for help to arrive and when it doesn't she
sighs. Then her hands reappear, she plays out several
attempts to free her nose, but as we're laughing
heartily she stays with her problem. "Right," she
says with determination, "now I AM going to do
something... I'm going!" Firmly holding the two
screens, her red nose still wedged between them,
she drags the screens awkwardly off stage. We are
still laughing and applauding when she finally
manages to disentangle herself and return to her
seat.

In another improvisation she paired up with a friend, whom she'd asked in advance to help her take breaks and pass the focus. They decided that an etiquette class would be the ideal situation for her clown, with her friend in the role of the tutor, offering advice and giving instructions on: how and when to talk, how and when to move, and of course, on making sure one's words and actions are inoffensive in polite society. The resulting improvisation was superb. Playing the low status role Pamela could follow her comic instincts, create problems and be as enthusiastic as she wanted, but with long breathing spaces marked by her friend, who politely, and with impeccable elegance, requested her to calm down or shut up.

These and other improvisations certainly helped her feel more comfortable tempering her usual manic resourcefulness, but she had yet to show how events could humble her; she still had not let us into her heart. This finally happened in a completely unexpected way, with an exercise we call, "Duty versus pleasure". In this exercise, we ask students to cross the stage with a certain amount of urgency. The urgency is due to an important pending appointment with "duty" (a job interview, a meeting with a bank manager for a loan, picking up the kids from school, etc.), but halfway there the clown sees an apple on a chair: "pleasure" calling. The clown must play out the dilemma between the call to "duty" (and all that s/he feels about that) and the call of "pleasure" (which is obviously infinitely more attractive), before resolving it one way or another.

When Pamela came forward to do the exercise, Alex suggested her duty be the first day in a new job. He insisted that the job was essential to her, because she needed money urgently, there was absolutely nothing left in her kitchen cupboards and her four year old son was hungry. (Such extreme situations are actually very necessary, without them the clown would see the apple and forget all about his/her duty in an instant). While Pamela listened to Alex's words, her expression indicated that she had first hand experience of being a mother with economic problems. Alex had unwittingly touched a sensitive spot within her, and this time there was no escaping it.

She began the improvisation with her usual high-spirited craziness, her comments and actions as hilarious as ever. She squeezed the dilemma for all it was worth before choosing to forget her duty. She sat on the chair, completely prepared to surrender to pleasure, her mouth just about to take a huge bite from the apple, when Alex activated the ring tone on his phone. When she answered the imaginary phone call, he said (imitating the voice of a child), "Mummy, where are you? I'm hungry." These words caught her completely off guard. For a long moment she didn't know what to say or how to react, she was immersed in a feeling of pure impotence.

That moment stilled us all, no-one even breathed; she had let us in, let us feel her vulnerability, and our hearts went out to her; she'd won over us completely. As Pamela sat back down among her companions in the audience, she recognised the importance of her experience, valuable not only for her clown but for herself. She knew that she'd found that moment of emptiness, and that it was much less scary than she'd imagined. Now she just had to take the definitive step; transform her feelings of powerlessness into a potent performance resource. She had to be ridiculously impotent and enjoy wallowing in it.

And of course, she did just that, in the very next exercise. "The object of your desire" (exercise 10, explained in chapter 12), was ideal, her perfect opportunity to play the victim. She entered the stage, saw the pink wig lying on the floor and instantly knew that with that wig she would become a Disco Superstar. She could be famous, sexy, happy, if it wasn't for those stupid lines fencing off the wig, that prevented her from grabbing it and realising her dreams. How frustrating! And there seemed to be absolutely nothing she could do...

Pamela played the situation as if she had lived a lifetime of powerlessness. She exaggerated an attitude of "poor little me" to ridiculous proportions, turning it into a double edged game. She played the victim so overtly that it became obvious that it was all just a manipulative strategy to get us to do things for her. Between her failed attempts to get the wig and her episodes of frustrated yearning, she asked us for help with trembling lips, and a weedy voice, "I can't do it by myself, I'm just not able to do it without help. Pleeaassee, pleeeasse, I beg you, heeeeelp meee." She looked at us like a lost puppy. It was so stupidly pathetic that, although we felt moved to reach out and help her, it didn't even cross our minds to actually do so, because that would have meant the end of her performance and our laughter.

The venture

Thomas Edison failed on over a thousand occasions before finally perfecting the first electric light bulb. A thousand times! Depending on how you look at it, this represents years of failure or years of moving towards a goal. Everything depends on your attitude to complicated or difficult tasks. Edison was a scientist, and scientists understand that in order to progress they have to test their theories by putting them into practice. Trial and error is an accepted part of the process, results are correlated and built upon until a successful result is achieved. Undoubtedly Edison felt frustrated at times, but that didn't put a dampener on his belief that a light bulb was possible. He is quoted as having said: "Many of life's failures are people who did not realise how close they were to success when they gave up."

I always try and make my beginner students understand that they shouldn't worry if they don't get an immediate, positive response from the audience; that instead they should continue their quest for the things that work. Increasingly I emphasize the fact that improvising is always a trial and error process, that they should be more scientific in their approach and avoid taking personally their unsuccessful attempts at being funny. "Keep looking" is a very encouraging recommendation for those who are having trouble finding what works for them, it helps them stay calm even when there's a deadly silence in the audience. I explain that what they are looking for is that one little something that will cause a first laugh or smile in the audience. They can try breaking the ice by offering something of themselves and, if it doesn't work, they should take a greater risk; be more stupid or foolish, exaggerate what they've done or try something completely new.

It is essential that they begin to see that they'll only get as far as they themselves are prepared to go, but that does not mean that they should force themselves to do better. In clowning, the opposite is required. Students are more likely to be successful if they don't put themselves under pressure, if they let go of a perfect outcome and simply explore. People who enroll in a clown course want to learn the art of being ridiculous. Few really know how to let themselves be ridiculous, but those brave enough to get out there and try will be all the encouragement the others need!

I always try to help them when they're floundering. Being out front makes it much easier to see what could be funny. I'll ask them challenging or provocative questions, make tongue-in-cheek remarks about what they've done, ask them to repeat with precision something they did, suggest new things to do, take on roles for them to interact with, nod encouragingly, order them about, etc. I'll either use the things that spring to mind based on my long experience as a teacher or, if I see that the person requires something completely made to measure, I'll invent something new on the spot.

As the facilitator I have a responsibility to be alert at all times to the prevailing energy in the room. When someone has attempted a series of actions and none of them have worked, the overall energy nosedives and everyone begins to feel the rising tension. When the audience is uncomfortable (both because they're witnessing someone else's discomfort and feeling their own frustration), it becomes even harder to make them laugh. Laughter acts as an energizer, it lifts people's spirits and awakens their senses. Therefore, when you're trying to get laughs, it's much easier if your audience is already in a lively and playful state.

That is why I'll sometimes step in. For example, I'll whisper to someone sitting next to me in the class, "I'll distract him by asking him questions so you can sneak behind the screen. Move it slowly forward and we'll see how he responds." Or

I pretend I don't understand anything and begin to openly discuss what I think I may have understood. Any idea will do, as long as it's aligned loosely with the reason the clown's given for being there, or is so outrageous that it will help them loosen up and play.

My intention is to nudge the clown out of his/her hiding place, inspire my students to be ridiculous, but if they need more, I'll coax, dupe, entice, entrap, flatter, mislead, seduce, and sweet-talk them into coming out to play. For example, I'll use my knowledge of foreign languages and converse with them in the one they can't speak. If they do understand me I'll start talking faster and faster, or mispronouncing words. I also make up words in their own language; for instance I might ask them "Will you please aboreta for us", speaking with such total conviction and naturalness that they often think there must be a gap in their vocabulary!

It's very easy to behave ridiculously when you find yourself in a predicament. Encountering difficulty is actually a life line for clown students but many shy away from such encounters. All my cajoling helps them step out of their safety zone and enter an unfamiliar (but not altogether unknown) territory, where they can experience their own ridiculousness with creativity rather than embarrassment. Normally, it's not something people do in public, but that's why it's so interesting and inspiring to those who are observing the process. When human beings find themselves in a tight spot they will naturally tap into their deepest resources; their survival instinct kicks in and they become more creative, intuitive, inventive, and proactive. This is precisely the sort of behaviour I'm trying to encourage: behaviour that's spontaneous, resourceful and authentic.

As an added enticement to letting their hair down and stepping off the diving board I sometimes find it necessary to use music when students are improvising. Music is a great motivator. Certain songs transform us momentarily; they make us bold, wild, energetic, sexy, etc... or at least that's what we think we're being! More often than not we're just acting ludicrously. I therefore have a large repertoire of music on hand, to use when the occasion calls. With the appropriate music, students who have been having problems letting themselves go will suddenly fling themselves into being rockers, rappers, heroes, belly dancers, sex kings and queens (etc.) with childlike enthusiasm. The results are often hilarious, and many students have afterwards related how flabbergasted they were by the amount or quality of energy they were able to access.

Trial and error

In reading this book or in your own practice, you have probably realised that clowning has its complexities, that it is a discipline that you have to learn over an extended period of time. However, a high percentage of my students get frustrated with themselves, even those who have quite a lot of experience under their belts. Why? Because they haven't fully registered that clowning is an art form, and as such demands long periods of practice and experimentation.

If you've ever tried playing an instrument, or painting a water colour or singing in a chorus you'll know that there's always a lot more to mastering an art than meets the eye. Since early childhood I have always been a voracious reader, but I never stopped to wonder why I liked one book and not another until I started writing this one. It was only when I found myself sitting in front of my laptop looking for my style — dredging the well of my ideas and memories and wondering how to give them form — that I suddenly began to see how much craft was involved. It wasn't just a question of putting words on paper; writing was about perception, meaning, feeling, rhythm, poetry, expression, soul. The experience of writing has given me a glimpse of the writer's art, and of course, my respect for professional authors has increased considerably. So has my humility; I have discovered how much there is still to learn.

So, when clowning, it's worth remembering that practice makes perfect but it takes years to perfect talent. For instance, you now walk with utter ease, but to confidently exhibit this skill you had to acquire a whole set of other skills first and you had to practise each stage in the process a thousand times, just to get that little bit nearer to your goal. To be able to raise yourself up and take your first steps, you first had to learn how to use your body and strengthen it. You had to learn how to roll over, sit, crawl, stand up, sit down from a standing position, balance on two feet, walk with support and finally find the courage and will power to take your first steps. And yet, even with all this practice, those steps were unstable and awkward.

In order to walk with the ease and coordination you now possess, you've fallen every which way a million times. But it's the knowledge you acquired about falling that gave you the confidence to continue pushing yourself to go further; to learn how to run and jump and climb, etc. The same applies when you're acquiring clowning skills. You have to learn that falling from grace is not as dramatic as it feels. If you're going to gain experience you simply have to try, try and try again. Take on learning one part of the technique, and then build on it. If you place too many demands on yourself, you'll only lose confidence rather than gain it. Self imposed standards of excellence are detrimental to clown training. "I'm going to make them laugh 'till they split their sides" is an extreme goal even for a professional; don't pile that kind of pressure on yourself. Everyone has their own rhythm, some will assimilate a skill quickly, others will need more time. By all means go for the "How pleasurable!" but don't be overly discouraged if you encounter the "How awful!" Among professional clowns it's a well known fact that it takes at least ten years of trial and error before one is able to do a decent job whatever the circumstances.

How did it go?

An important component to the initial work I do with my students is audience awareness. It's crucial that they know if what they are doing is working or not for their audience, which means habitually checking the response they're getting, not just ploughing on regardless. I encourage them to use their eyes and their ears to receive feedback from individual members of their audience. If someone is smiling, they've got a friend; if someone's laughing, he or she is their ally; and if various people are laughing, they've been granted a license to go for it. Any of these reactions should be interpreted as a success; a small success, a medium success, or a big success.

A major problem students have in the early stages of clowning is information overload. Performing for an audience is such a novelty that they find it hard to process all the information they're receiving. Their five sense are working overtime, how then can they possibly take in what the audience is doing as well? The feeling is similar to taking your first driving lesson. There seem to be far too many things to be aware of at the same time. In clowning, the easiest way to check on the audience is to take a moment's pause, stop all other activity and focus on them. It's particularly important to do this when you've completed a sequence or routine, come to the end of a paragraph so to speak, because you can use the pause to share; to show the audience how you feel about what you've just done, see how they feel about it and react to their response.

I use a very simple exercise to develop this particular skill. The exercise allows students to feel and see how important (and funny) the dynamic of pausing and sharing can be. I ask students to choose an emotion and tell them that 'the show' they have to perform is as follows: they must enter playing the emotion they have chosen, come to the centre of the stage and within that same emotion say, "Hello, my name is... and the earth is round." During 'the show' they can have as much fun as they want to, they can try things and if they don't work, try other things. The only condition is that when it's all done they have to take a long pause and show us how they feel about what happened and the response they got from the audience.

Having such a simple task to complete doesn't mean they'll remember to do the final assessment on themselves, more often than not I have to step in and remind them to share their perceptions. "How did the show go?" I ask them from the sidelines. Many opt for the easy way out at this point. However, saying "bad" or "good", without providing any further information is not enough, and answering, "fine" when their show was a disaster, or "terrible" when they actually did well, is even less productive. The audience will feel bored, confused or misled by such responses so the students need to be redirected to use more creative responses.

"Fine?" I ask. "It was terrible! A three year old could have done better." I'm not trying to destroy them, just coach them into reacting from their clown — stop denying their failure and start living it.

"Terrible?" I say. "Is there anyone here who laughed?" Hands in the audience go up. Again, I'm trying to provoke a more honest reaction, get them to stop denying their success and begin enjoying it.

The more creatively comic they are in their reactions the better. This becomes even more important when they've just done something that has flopped. I teach a three step process to follow that I call "absorbing failure". Absorbing failure begins with the recognition that something has failed; the clown then feels the failure internally (admitting vulnerability), before externalizing the feeling and playing with it. Obviously there is an endless number of ways to live this process, some very subtle, others not at all. The situation the clown finds him/herself in when failure strikes will affect how s/he reacts. Accordingly, the flop might feel huge or funny or inevitable. The emotional response is the starting point; what can be made of it is up to each individual's creativity. Here are some ways I've seen failure played out:

It was a disaster and the protagonist:

- starts a monologue of excuses, each one more ridiculous than the one before: the lights are too bright, the stage is not flat, the curtains are too colourful, the audience too beautiful, etc.
- doesn't understand what went wrong (and desperately tries to understand by breaking down the failure into infinitesimal parts).
- denies the disaster, in ever more vigorous and emphatic ways.
- rebels against authority; us, the rules, the regulations, the laws about this and that, expectations, repression, etc.
- bursts into uncontrollable laughter, and makes no attempt to control it.
- acknowledges that he's having a bad day, the alarm clock didn't go off, he got out of bed on the wrong side, he burnt his toast, etc.

- maintains a buoyant enthusiasm for what she just did, even repeating the flop because she really is convinced that the gag is great.
- remains relaxed because he's cool and of-course it really is 'no problem'.
- plays the absolute victim, wallowing in the failures of her life, of the world, of humanity.
- becomes filled with doubt. "Was it a flop? No, surely not! But then again... maybe... "
- becomes angry with himself, "You fool! What an idiot you are! I'm going to beat you up! Coward, do not shrink from this, you deserve it."
- commences a therapy session, assuming the roles of both therapist and patient.
- feels physical pain. "Oh how it hurts... in my heart... no, it's my stomach... what agony! No the pain's in my heart *and* my stomach... and maybe in my left eyebrow too... "
- becomes extremely nervous. She develops an un-controllable twitch, tries to relax but fails, which provokes an even more evident twitch somewhere else.
- is overwhelmed by guilt — "How could I have done that? It was absolutely terrible. I'll never be able to forgive myself. It was all my fault."

The Corner

The idea of creating a completely new dimension to the children's games that are played in clown class came about several years ago. The Loser's Corner was a solution Alex and I came up with to the normal response to losing, which was typically to abandon the game altogether, with no opportunity for a comeback. The unquestioned implication was that eliminated players no longer play; they become losers, and being a loser means becoming a passive observer.

Obviously this felt totally out of keeping with the rest of the clown pedagogy we were teaching, where losers could still have fun and be creative, that's why we invented a place within the workspace for losers. The same basic rules applied to the games, players still got eliminated and had to leave, but instead of retiring altogether from the fun, they went to 'The Loser's Corner'. Once there they were able to remain active and participatory and could even return to the game if their clown could find a way to do so (pleading with authority, tricking another to take their place, entering the game to point out another's fault, changing an aspect of their clothing in an attempt to fool authority, etc.). In this way losers learn to keep the game of failing alive and interesting, and everyone wins, in that entertainment can be offered and experienced by all.

Another positive result is that students learn that a clown never gives up in the face of adversity and always remains hopeful. If, as clowns, they are ordered to leave the stage, because they're not needed or wanted, they can remain light-hearted. Clowns, love being on stage so they'll never give up trying to return. They'll either suffer from a memory relapse or forget on purpose, because that "Get out!" wasn't really meant to be taken seriously, no way! 'Surely,' they think, 'it is only a matter of waiting a bit, or disguising myself with a false moustache, or entering the stage from the other side, or making the most of a moment when nothing important seems to be happening. The boss will have forgotten what happened or won't recognise me, he may even laugh.'

So now, when I introduce a new game I will not only explain how to play it but I will also, as part of the rules, designate a specific place in the room where students have to go once they've messed up. I always choose a place along a side wall, not an actual corner, so that the losers are visible to those who are still playing. I tell them that once they're in The Loser's Corner they're still playing as clowns, just as those who are still in the game, which means everyone needs to stay aware of what's happening, both in The Corner and within the game. The losers need to respect the focus and listen to the voice of authority (me) in order to avoid chaos, but they can use their wit and wits to find ways of participating.

One of my favourite games with a Loser's Corner is 'Group Creation'. As with most children's games, in essence it is very simple, but, with the addition of The Corner, I've witnessed some extraordinary clowning. The game is as follows:

All the players move about the space until the teacher shouts out, "Groups of 2... 3, 4, 5, 6". The number that is chosen takes into account how many players are circulating at any given time. There must always be more players in the game than multiples of the number announced (for example: if there are thirteen players the teacher calls out, "groups of four"). Players have to form the groups quickly, those who have no group to join must leave the game and go to The Loser's Corner, but they are given the focus until the teacher resumes the game.

I make everyone lose by asking the last player to form a group of three, and as this is impossible, they too have to join the rest in The Corner. However, the students don't know this. I find it fascinating to observe the many ways they'll try to avoid being eliminated. Unwittingly, they reveal what drives them and how they feel about losing. Suddenly they become unabashedly competitive, desperate, angry or confused. Or other attributes will surface, such as their sense of fair play, their compassion or their generosity. I take a keen note of all this information, as it gives me vital clues about where to go in helping them discover their clown.

I have learnt that it makes for a much safer game if I explain that physical aggression is completely unnecessary. In the frantic scrambling that occurs when groups are formed, participants sometimes bordered on the dangerous; jumping wildly onto people's backs, pushing or pulling individuals out of the group, etc. Consequently, before starting the game, I always clarify the real reason for playing games: to discover things about their clowns. I underscore the need for creative solutions; that it's far more interesting, if there are too many members to a group, that the individuals within it reach an agreement on who is to leave. They can do this by exchanging glances or through simple movements (such as gently patting someone on the back or moving an arm to exclude them from the group). The "chosen one" has to accept the group's decision, though this doesn't mean they have to do it graciously!

Without hostility the game becomes much more amusing and engaging for everyone concerned. I've often been surprised by the tenderness and solidarity that clowns will demonstrate in that delicate moment of deciding who has got to go. A great example of this happened during a course Alex Navarro and I gave in Portugal some years ago. The game was well under way when Alex shouted, "groups of three". As always, one group was too large, containing four members instead of three. Almost instantly, one of the clowns decided that he would be the one to sacrifice himself, but when he tried to leave the other three grabbed hold of him, "Don't leave, pleaseeee, don't leave!" they begged him. The clown who had decided to leave sighed and, with an expression of deep resignation, delicately disengaged himself from the others. He took a step towards The Loser's Corner but his group, as one entity, quickly moved to surround him again, repeating their pleas: "don't go, please, don't leave us!" He looked at Alex and I questioningly, 'What was he to do?', but we weren't going to solve his problem, it was far too interesting.

He was stoically determined on his course of action so he kept trying to move towards The Loser's Corner but his clown companions kept finding new ways to prevent him from getting there: they threw themselves at his feet, they interlinked their arms to form a barrier, they blew at him as hard as they could. All four clowns moved with measured gentleness, thereby reinforcing the affection for each other they had expressed vocally. This touching scene had everyone in the room spell bound, each new development feeding our general delight. However, they had to find a resolution that was on a par with the rest of their performance; fortunately, they didn't disappoint us.

At our insistence, that someone had to leave the game, the trio looked at each other and nodded. Then they each warmly embraced the clown who had been trying to leave. "Goodbye," they said, before turning their backs on him and walking proudly towards The Corner, "we'll be waiting for you!" And just before stepping over the line, they each turned and extended a final salute to their friend and the rest of the players. An explosion of applause accompanied them as they stepped into The Corner. We all knew we had just been given a clown masterclass on the inspiring and uplifting effects of adopting an altruistic attitude towards failure.

9
Game-playing strategies

Playing is first and foremost about having fun; that is it's only true purpose. And, as you by now know, having fun is what clowns are all about. Play, or the sense of play, is therefore vital at all stages in clown training but it is also incredibly important to preserve as a professional. Clown improvisations and performances are based on game playing and play, not least because people laugh more easily when given a comic stimulus which is obviously playful in tone. However, as in all clown technique, there is a lot more to the clown's game playing than at first meets the eye.

My students' initial ability to play and have fun varies enormously, and their age is not the determining factor (in fact it's often the over sixties students who more readily throw themselves into games). Sadly, all too many of the people who attend my courses stopped playing very early on in life and their sense of play is often rusty to say the least. Therefore, I always start with simple children's games just to help them remember how it feels to play inconsequentially. Normally I kick off with a game of tag.

I am always amazed at how this game can transport everyone immediately into a parallel reality. Right from the start, every single adult in the room is running around and squealing or laughing, making mad dashes from one end of the room to the other, dodging and diving, even risking falling on their faces in their urgency not to be tagged. None of them is questioning the game or its rules, nor do they think about its foolishness or their own, nor are they asking themselves, "Why is not getting tagged so important to me?" Clearly all their normal intellectual deliberations are swept aside as they instinctively channel all their efforts into avoiding being "it". And no-one ever willingly wants to be "it". It's as if they're all thinking in unison, 'if anyone's going to be a loser, it's not me!' No-one reflects that someone has *got* to be a loser for the game to work at all.

From the outside I see the game has displaced their normal reserve and as a result they're all more agile, fluid, and funny. That is precisely why it's so important that they recover their ability to play before attempting anything on stage, an ability which returns the minute they actually start playing.

Once they've loosened up in this very basic way they're ready to play other games that are fun but that also induce concentration, trust, spontaneity and awareness. These are all essential qualities for playing most games but are especially necessary when playing clown games. Students have got to "get warm" which means waking up completely; mentally, physically and energetically. And, if they're playing with others, they also need to be on a similar wave-length and feel a certain level of trust towards the other players. As the morning progresses everyone's playful nature slowly reawakens and I begin to see flashes of clown-like behaviour breaking out spontaneously in all directions. When this happens I know they are ready to take the plunge and play as clowns for an audience.

At this point it's useful for them to be told that playing for an audience is fascinatingly complicated until it becomes second nature. Then, and only then, does it look deceptively easy. Many first time students in my workshops are natural clowns but even they need to learn the basic strategies involved in initiating, improvising and staging games for an audience. These strategies are, in reality, more like orientation signs that point students in the right direction but never limit their freedom of choice. They help maintain clarity, simplicity and rapport whilst playing, which as I've already stated, are major comedy cornerstones.

Inner joy

In this and the next chapter I have detailed these strategies so that you can apply them in your own work. However, I feel I should first stress the importance of you finding your inner joy when playing, off or on stage. If you observe children playing imaginative games or, better still, actually play these inventive games with them, you'll soon find out that the pursuit of pleasure is the real reason for playing them.

My daughter, throughout her childhood, was always happiest when playing and she was therefore a keen player and a great inventor of games. When she enjoyed a particular game she would keep returning to it, reinventing it slightly to keep it interesting, but keeping the basic structure intact, unless that too got reinvented by a new imaginative leap. She would love inventing rules for her games, especially those based on role play in which I would participate.

"You're the monster and you capture me", she'd start,
but as soon as I attempted to do so she'd run away.
"Hey, I'm supposed to capture you!" I'd growl.

*"I've found an invisible cloak, you can't see me!"
she'd reply whilst sneaking behind me and jumping onto my back.
"Something's just landed on me, but I can't see what
it is", I'd grunt whilst whirling around in a fake
attempt to shake her off. She'd squeal with delight
and find endless ways to prolong the fun.
One day, whilst playing the bad monster game, I
dragged out a pile of imaginary chains and locked
her in a deep, dark dungeon under the covers on her
bed.
"Now", I said triumphantly, "you will never escape
and I will eat you for dinner!"
But once again she outsmarted me. She simply spat
out an imaginary key (sneakily hidden there at some
prior moment), hastily unlocked herself and ran off
shrieking with laughter, "Sorry Monster, you'll just
have to eat vegetables tonight!"*

As this shows, children will always change a game to suit
themselves. They don't have to have this explained to them, it
comes naturally, but we adults need to be reminded: the key
to successful playing is our own inner joy. The question to ask
yourself, therefore, if you ever get stuck for a game to play on
stage is: "What would I like to do now?" Surprisingly simple,
isn't it?

"In Spymonkey we identify the games we want
to play and how we like playing them but every
performance is a new adventure in discovery.
Even when we've consolidated the show we keep
playing. If there's no risk, there's no fun. As a
clown you have to give yourself the permission

to not plan ahead. The motor, the fuel, the elixia of your performance is always your pleasure."

Aitor Basauri, Spymonkey, Spain/England

Finding the game

Your clown teacher asks for a volunteer, you step forwards. She then explains the exercise. You take in what you are supposed to do, and walk back stage in order to begin. You put on your nose and think about how to start and all of a sudden you realise that once again you're standing on the edge of a diving board with a blindfold on, about to leap into thin air. The exercise is only the starting point, the diving board, but in reality the game has not been fixed, you still have to find the game your clown plays for the audience.

Finding a game to play is not as difficult as it first seems. Gradually you will discover that there are an endless amount of games for your clown to play. Often the hardest part is actually recognizing the game that you've already begun, the moment you walk out onstage. Being open and alert will definitely help you, but the easiest way is through listening to your audience's reactions. They will tell you (not only by their laughter or silence but also by their physical posture or energy levels) when a game has started, when they want more of the same game or when a game stops working for them.

Sometimes, as I've said, a game will start spontaneously because your clown has walked out onstage with you. However, if your connection with your clown is faulty, which it will be at different times throughout your training, you will have to initiate something simple, a gesture, an action or an emotional state, and watch for a positive reaction, either inside yourself or from the audience.

The initiation of something new is a proposal, your clown proposing a new game. A clown can turn anything into a game but the best game proposals are the ones that are both clear and engaging. Also, the stronger your proposal and the easier it is to appreciate without serious intellectual effort, the better. The audience has got to be able to see and connect with the initial proposal in order to follow your imaginative thread, relax and laugh. Proposals which define how you feel, what you're doing onstage, what interests you, where you are or what your relationship is to the people or objects around you will all also give you something solid with which to play. And if what you propose happens to be funny, then you really know you're on the right track!

Good game proposals are therefore meaty (with substance) or juicy (appetizing). They guide you forwards with ease because they're like a beacon that illuminates the way ahead. Bad proposals are the ones that don't inspire further creativity; the ones that don't have enough emotional force to suck you in or are just too bland to be interesting. You usually make weak proposals when you're not being honest or generous. Don't forget that the *how* is as important, if not more so, than the *what*. How you breathe or feel or move, how you say what you say, how you manifest your sense of humour, these particulars are most likely to be what the audience actually enjoys.

Sometimes you will find a game you can keep playing for the duration of your improvisation; at other times you'll have to change the game, either because the audience has lost interest, or because you have, which usually is one and the same thing. Sometimes there's only so far you can take a game before it naturally plays itself out, at others you'll find games within the game that will enrich the initial game structure no end. Below I've attempted to clarify all this with examples. These examples I have taken from students' improvisations over the years. It's always hard do justice to a clown's performance through the written word, so much of the humour gets lost without the visual stimulation, but I've tried my best.

In some examples below I have included the remarks I made to help floundering students. My input is often a vital lifeline for beginner and intermediate students, but as much as possible, I try to let them discover for themselves and encourage them to incorporate my suggestions without interrupting the flow of their improvisations. However, there are occasions when I make students leave the stage to recommence their improvisation. This happens either because their energy levels need readjusting, or because they have not understood the exercise, or because they've started off on such a bad footing that continuing would inevitably mean going from bad to worse.

Exercise 1: What game are we playing?

Two clowns. The first enters, makes contact with the audience and starts something small or allows something to capture their interest. The second enters from the opposite side, makes contact with the audience, and then notices the other clown. They do not already know each other. If something starts naturally, they should go with it, but until it does they should simply pay attention and let themselves feel. As soon as they capture a game proposal, either their own or their partner's, they should accept it, find ways to reinforce or support it, and play it out to the full.

Example:

Frank enters the stage enthusiastically and, upon reaching centre stage, looks about him as if drinking up the world. First he takes in the stage area, "Wow!"; then he takes in the overhead lighting, "Wow!" again; and then the audience, "Wow!"; followed by a big smile.

The audience laughs. He's already started a game but he is not aware of having done so.

His partner, Lucy, enters stage and looks around with tenderness and affection. With the same expression she takes in Frank. Frank doesn't know how to react.

I side coach: Frank, "Wow!"

Frank acts on the stimulus and says, "Wow!" enthusiastically. They then run into each others arms and embrace.

Side coaching: No, go back to where you were, four meters distance from each other. Remember: If you get together instantly you have thrown away the whole game, the game of your mutual attraction and how that attraction makes you act. You haven't allowed yourselves the opportunity to explore the crazy ideas you'll get, ideas about how to seduce each other and get close.

They go back to their original distance. Frank takes up a body builder's pose and turns towards her, his whole body on display.

Side coaching: No, have the idea first. Think: maybe being more macho might be effective in seducing her. First show her your arm, see how she reacts.

Frank does this and gets a laugh. Lucy shows she is interested.

Side coaching: Now the other arm Frank. Take it step by step and don't forget to show us how you both feel every time, let the attraction mount.

They do this and the game works well. The audience is enjoying it so much they want more but Frank and Lucy don't hear this and think the game has ended. Once again they run into a mutual embrace.

Side coaching: No. Now it's her turn. What do you think will be attractive to him Lucy? What's your seduction ritual?

Lucy shows us her feminine charms in a very ridiculous way. Frank responds to each of her actions with an enthusiastic, "Wow!" The audience is loving it.

Side coaching: Yes! Now, Frank, start exaggerating the "wow", play with how you say it so that it turns into a kind of mating call.

Frank does this too, very effectively. It works so well that Lucy is encouraged to try her own mating call. Frank gets to say "Wow" again.

Ten minutes have gone by and they can still get so much out of the game. From here they could take the audience through their first dance, the moment leading up to their first kiss, the kiss itself, their reaction to the kiss, his attempt to whisk her off her feet (literally or otherwise), her attempt to do the same, their mounting desire to be alone, how they get off stage without losing their physical contact and the "Wow!" we hear once they're out of sight, but this time from both of them in unison.

Saying "Yes"

As you can see in the above example, recognizing that the game has already started is vital when playing on stage. When the audience sees that you've got something that works, they won't want you to change the game straight away or, worse, just throw it away. What they want is to see you play the game, detail by detail, develop your initial game proposals in unexpected ways. If you don't learn how to do this, you'll find yourself in the awful position of having to find endless new games to play and never having any fun.

I know, from watching students struggle to understand how to stretch out games on stage, that many of them don't find it easy. There seems to be a generalized tendency to jump ahead, to not stay with the game, simply because they don't understand how funny all the details can be. The details are precisely where the comedy lies. This is why the emotional as well as the physical content of every game has to be played out fully, one step at a time.

So that is the first thing I try and get my students to assimilate: that smaller steps are required along with a whole-hearted inner "yes!" This "yes!" is both an acceptance of what has been proposed and a decision to throw yourself 100% into the game. Your complete involvement in the game will make it much easier for you to play out the details, they'll come to you without effort, especially with a little practice.

Complete involvement implies a state of presence, of being absolutely present to what is happening and how it makes you feel. Many students are already able to do this naturally with no help from me, but in general they need to understand the ways in which they are blocking or avoiding being fully present. Below are a few golden rules that really help:

- Say "yes!" to all proposals.
- Listen actively.
- Stay interested and curious.
- Make your own decisions (do not ask questions like "What are you doing?" or "Why are you doing that?").
- Keep in contact (eye contact, sense contact).
- Don't panic if things don't work straight away.

In the following exercise notice how the clowns are applying all these rules and what a remarkable difference they make in the creation of the game.

Exercise 2: Shipwrecked
Four or five clowns. It is explained that the night before there was a tremendous storm at sea. The ship on which the clowns were travelling, sunk. They are the survivors, washed up on a deserted beach of an unknown island. At the start of the improvisation they are still unconscious, lying on the floor. The first

to stir is the ship's captain. S/he is duty bound to get the others organised and explore the island for a means by which they can be rescued. (I use a tropical beach sound-track only at the start to set the scene).

Example:
The Captain is having nightmares about the previous night. Her movements and scrambled screams make the others stir in their sleep. She sits bolt upright with a loud gurgle. The others judder awake and stand up slowly. They naturally huddle together, forlornly looking about them. The Captain is also looking about her despondently but on seeing the audience she shakes it off, squaring her shoulders against despair.

Captain: Sailors! Pull yourselves together. Every man to his task. You! Keep a look out over the water, there may be giant crocodiles. You! Watch the jungle, the wild boars are extremely dangerous in these parts. And you! Watch the sky, there'll be hungry pterodactyls flying nearby.

The sailors begin to tremble with fear as they form a triangle, backs together, each one looking in a different direction. Their paranoia is obvious. The sailor looking out towards the audience (and the sea) suddenly freezes with terror.

Sailor 1: (*with a faint voice*) Captain. Captain!

The Captain is busy, ear to the floor, listening for oncoming perils.

Sailor 1: Captain, a...

The Captain pretends not to have heard this and moves towards the water looking at an animal track. She compares her own feet to the print then measures it with hand spans, it's huge.

Sailor 1: Captain, a giant crocodile!

The Captain sees the crocodile and fearlessly jumps forwards, miming a fight with the beast. She struggles across the stage in a heroic attempt to get the upper hand.

C: Help me out here sailors!

The sailors turn to face each other and exchange urgent looks.

Sailor 1: You go.

Sailor 2: No, you go.

Sailor 3: Me? Why me? It's not fair.

This continues for awhile, none of them wanting to put themselves at risk. Suddenly one of them changes tactics, becoming extremely polite.

Sailor 2: No, really, it is extremely kind of you, but I can assure you that I do not mind. Please go first.

The other two join in instantly.

Sailor 3: No, no, no, I would never forgive myself if I took all the lime light when <u>you</u> can do so much a better job. Please, go ahead I'll be right behind you.

Sailor 1: Oh, I would love to see <u>you</u> being the hero of the day, you deserve it, really.

Meanwhile the Captain has opened the crocodile's mouth. She's holding its jaws wide open but the effort is becoming too much for her.

C: Hey! What the hell are you up to? All for one and one for all. That's an order!

The Sailors exchange looks of resignation. One by one they put their hands behind their backs.

Sailor 3: Paper, stone or scissors. 1, 2, 3, go!

They each pull out a different object so that all of them win against another.

C: (*she's losing the fight*) I can't hold on any longer... ahhhh!

She mimes being eaten by the crocodile. The sailors rush to save her, forming a line on the floor each holding the boots of the other. The first sailor grabs the Captain's feet.

Sailor 1: Don't worry, Captain, everything's going to turn out just fine. All for one, just like you said.

But instead of pulling the Captain backwards they all slide forwards, each one getting eaten by the crocodile. They end up in a pile together.

C: Idiots!

The sailors repeat the last two syllables of the Captain's word as if there was an impressive echo in the crocodile's stomach.

Sailors: iots... iots... iots.

They roll out of the pile and sit in a line facing the audience.

Sailor 2: It's really dark in here.

Sailor 3: Yes, I can't see a thing.

Sailor 1: I've got an idea Captain! We could sing a lullaby. The crocodile will fall asleep and when he opens his mouth to snore we'll be able to escape.

C: Let's give it a try, sailor. I haven't a better idea.

They begin to sway slowly from side to side as they invent a lullaby, taking turns to sing. As the forth sings his line, he begins to yawn, the others follow suit, yawning and letting their eyes droop. One by one they fall into a sleepy heap, snoring their lullaby.

Explain the why's

I have already mentioned that clowns act logically. There is always a reason behind what they do, even if it is a clown's reason. Acting logically is incredibly important, but again, it seems to be something that does not come naturally to people. My students struggle with the why's of their actions so much that it's made me understand why the world is such a crazy place!

Why do you move forwards? Why have you made that gesture? Why that look? Why are you feeling happy now when only a moment ago you were sad?

These are the questions audiences will ask, even if only inside their heads. If you don't help them understand the why's you'll lose them, they simply won't be able to follow you. On stage the why's of all you do have to be so clear that nobody needs to ask questions. Again, this is basic stage craft and another comedy cornerstone.

The why's are what motivates or justifies any action, "I'm hot so I'll take off my jumper". We understand the action if we know the reasoning behind it (however crazy it might be). Training yourself to explain your motives without effort or even conscious thought will take time. But the expression of the clown's internal logic can be so helpful when creating comedy that you'll soon see the value in identifying it. Becoming aware of the times you haven't acted logically is a first step. You've just lost your audience, could it be that they haven't understood a why? Why *did* you move five steps forward? If you can catch the illogical movement and explain it, I swear, the audience will think you're a genius!

So ask yourself what could justify your action. This shouldn't make you tense or hesitant, it's just a part of the game. Why did you move forwards? Often the *way* you did it will give you the answer. Did you stride, walk nonchalantly, tiptoe? Did you swagger or were you shy? Did you feel uncomfortable with where you were or were you attracted by something you saw?

Really, all I'm saying is that in becoming more aware of the logic behind your action, your next move will come to you without effort (it'll be a follow-through of what you just did), and the improvisation will move forwards with explicable ease. Your team-mates will feel at ease too, because you'll not be asking *them* to interpret your actions for you. You may even get so skilled in this that you can help them out of an illogical moment by instantly offering a why for their odd behaviour! The following example highlights this skill and hopefully shows how funny it can prove to be.

Exercise 3: The object shop
This is a remix of similar clown exercises, where clowns are asked to explain to the audience extraordinary make-believe inventions or the amazing versatility of ordinary objects.

Three clowns. One plays the boss, the other two, assistants. They're asked to present, in front of an important group of buyers, the objects that they have brought with them to the class. They must first explain the inventions and their use before trying to sell them. The assistants are instructed to create problems for their boss.

Example:
Victor, Martha and Cynthia come on together. They look like a group of hippy friends, slightly high. Victor is in the middle and takes the initiative, assuming the role of authority.

Victor: We've come to sell weapons. New generation, high-tech weapons for advanced warfare.

Martha makes a pistol with her fingers and sexily imitates the sound of a gun shot.

M: Piao, piao.

Victor looks at her with perplexity but, on turning back to the audience, recovers his composure with a false little laugh.

V: Ha, ha. That's Martha, my wonderful assistant. Thank you Martha for kick starting us today. I can see our buyers are raring to go now! Well, let us begin shall we? Martha, why don't you go and get the first weapon?

Martha is trying out Laura Croft type poses.

(Martha isn't listening to or playing with the others. She's immersed in her own game. Victor is left to resolve the situation.)

He turns to Cynthia who is smiling stupidly at the audience. She's got a hand inside her overcoat. On seeing this Victor takes up a defensive James Bond pose. Cynthia doesn't react.

(She's not listening to his proposals either. Now Victor has a REAL problem, it's up to him to explain all the why's.)

Cynthia pulls out a pair of rabbit ears attached to a headband from inside her coat. (Victor obviously didn't expect this but he instantly incorporates the strange action.)

V: Wow, you were amazingly quick there! I did not even see you leave to get it. What a wonderful team we make! Let's high five!

Victor tries to do this with Cynthia but she's been distracted by some movement in the audience and Marta is still lost in her own fantasies. She's mimicking a superheroine, pulling out all sorts of weapons from different parts of her anatomy.

(Victor is left looking stupid with his hands in the air, but once again finds a way out.)

He looks at both women and then puts his hands together in prayer. After a brief petition for strength and patience he high fives with God. Cynthia has refocused on Victor and imitates his last action.

(Victor reacts seamlessly, accepting her action and giving it logic.)

He turns and high fives with her but grabs the headband out of her hand. He looks at the audience with his false little laugh but this time it sounds even falser.

V: What synchronicity! What incredible precision! Just like the weapon I have here. Created in Switzerland and perfected in secret by our underground agents in Playboy.

(He's explained the why of the rabbit ears.)

He puts the headband on. Immediately Cynthia is fascinated by the movement of the rabbit ears. She moves close and follows attentively all of Victors' head movements, mimicking everything he does. Martha, whose own imagination has run its course, looks over at the two of them and instinctively moves closer, imitating Victor's movements from the other side.

(Victor, who was beginning to run through the amazing uses of the weapon on his head, becomes aware of his partners' movements and closeness. He does not break the moment but offers a logical explanation for it.)

V: As you can see, this is high tech at it's best. What you have here is an antenna that captures enemy movement and emits a signal that lures them to you.

Victor becomes conscious that the more he moves his head the more the audience laugh. He duly moves his head from side to side, then bends his legs to add a vertical movement to the horizontal. His partners mirror his moves in a trance state, inching closer until they are only a few centimeters from the ears. Victor begins to slow down his words and movements. The three of them playing in slow motion is hilarious. As soon as the laughter begins to die a little, Victor — still in slow motion — looks suspiciously from one to the other. Once again, for the audience, he laughs without any real humor then snaps his fingers in both their faces.

(Having played out the follow-the-leader game he returns to the structural logic of the improvisation: he's the boss and they're selling weapons).

V: Hey, don't let the power of this antenna give you a complete brain wash. Distance yourselves from its toxic waves! Why don't you go and get the second weapon while I turn this one off?

Neither of them react, both remain where they are, transfixed by the rabbit ears.

(Victor pauses to see if they are going to offer anything more. They don't. Once again he saves the situation by offering the next set of logical actions.)

He takes the ears off and waves them slowly from side to side in front of their faces.

> V: Team, liven up! Go get the next weapon! We have clients!
>
> *Cynthia and Martha finally liven up but they are still fixated on the ears. Victor seizes the opportunity and throws the headband towards the wings. It disappears out of sight with Cynthia and Martha chasing after it like two frisky dogs.*
>
> *(The audience explodes with laughter. Victor's talent at making a whole lot of craziness make sense is a lesson to them all.)*

How to develop game proposals

So, once started, the all important thing to do is develop the game, stretch it out, play it for all it's worth. Easy to say but not always obvious how you do it, as I've said. Experience is certainly an important factor but, as a beginner, there are three fundamental things you can do to help your clown develop games and keep them fluid and funny.

1. Find the pretext

One of the first things you should try to discover or define as soon as you can is: What is your pretext for being on stage?

Why are you here? What is it you want to show us? What's your objective? Have you come to do a job or pursue an obsession?

A pretext offers you a definite direction in which to head. Either it will inspire a series of logical actions that lead to the completion of your objective or it'll give you something concrete to play with while you blatantly avoid the task you have supposedly set out to do! Again it should be something simple but don't forget, even though it's simple doesn't mean your clown will find it easy to achieve!

Sometimes the exercise you'll be asked to improvise will give you a clear pretext or objective and so you won't have to spend time looking for one. Others are more open plan: see them as opportunities to find your own reasons for being on stage. You will soon find that defining these reasons (or reason) as early as possible in an improvisation will help you relax, play towards a known goal and give you a perfect way to end the action.

Remember: Clowns will actually find endless reasons for being on stage because they love the attention. The reasons flash before their eyes or leap out at them with an importance that in most cases is laughable. Like the reasons children offer to avoid bedtime, a clown's reasons for being on stage aren't life or death reasons, they're just excuses for staying a while longer in the limelight of their audience's gaze.

Exercise 4: 1, 2, 3, action!
The first time I saw this exercise was at a Funambules workshop performance. I have used this exercise to teach a wide range of clown techniques but it has been especially useful for working on recognizing and accepting game proposals, finding a pretext and enjoying mistakes.

A chair is placed downstage, centre. Two clowns. They are facing the back wall, some two meters' distance from each other, eyes closed and in a neutral posture.

In turn, still facing the wall, they must first announce out loud what they will do or say, then count (also out loud) 1, 2, 3, then perform the announced actions or sentences.

I recommend they do not announce more than three actions at a go to start with, unless they feel very confident that they will remember all they have said. They are also reminded of the importance of the emotional content and that they should announce it along with their physical actions, e.g. "I am going to open my eyes, turn towards the audience with resignation and when I see them I will sigh deeply."

They take turns announcing, counting and performing, keeping still when it's the others' turn but remaining fully present. However, they must return to the back wall if they forget to count 1, 2, 3 out loud, or do something they did not announce, or make a mistake in the order of their actions. The teacher can intervene if mistakes are made which the students don't acknowledge (this happens frequently!)

The aim of the clowns is to reach the chair first and sit down on it. When this happens the sitting clown has "won" and the improvisation ends. The clowns should not do this directly. They must first make contact with the audience and with their partner, start a game (either using the chair as a starting point or not), and finally, find logical reasons for moving towards the chair and sitting on it.

In this exercise even the initial turn towards the audience can be made into a game. I have seen some clowns enter the labyrinth of ways to make a turn and never get out; "I'm going to turn to face the audience", "I'm going to spin around", "I'm going to turn right around", "I'm going to turn to the right", "I'm going to do a half turn", "I'm going to turn 180°", "I'm going to do an arabesque turn", etc. They had no need of the chair but the game was played out to the full and everyone had fun all the same.

Example:
Peter announces he will open his eyes and turn to face the audience. He counts 1, 2, 3 and turns.

Gloria does the same.

Peter announces he will raise his arms. He counts and does so.

Gloria wants to take three strides forwards but forgets to count and returns to the wall.

Peter doesn't know what to do.

Side coaching: You've got your arms in the air, now you've got to do something related with that.

Peter: I'm going to move towards my partner.

Side coaching: No. First, do or say something to make us understand why you raised your arms. Moving towards Gloria won't help us understand.

Peter: I raised my arms so that Gloria could tickle my armpits.

Side coaching: That doesn't make sense. You raised your arms in an automatic way, without even looking at Gloria.

Peter: Because I perceived, out of the corner of my eye, that the person on my left is about to mug me, I raised my arms in automatic surrender. Now I am going to tremble a little and plead for my life.

(The audience laughs for the first time when he says this and again when he trembles and pleads.)

Side coaching: Yes! Direct, logical and funny. Great!

(Now the game has a clear direction to go in, both of them now know what their pretext for being on stage is).

Gloria turns and proceeds by stealing Peter's wallet which she places in her own pocket.

Side coaching: Is there nothing of interest in the wallet? Show us what you find.

Gloria opens the wallet, finds a banknote and acts pleased.

Peter: Now that she has what she wants I hope she will go away.

Side coaching: What about the game? Isn't there something more that could happen?

Peter: Since she is obviously a half wit and hasn't discovered my secret pocket full of cash I will breathe a sigh of relief.

(Again the audience laughs because the game has once again become interesting.)

Gloria: Now that I've discovered that being bad has it's advantages I am going to hold up the audience.

(Even though Gloria gets a laugh for this idea she has effectively ignored Peter and killed the game between them.)

Side coaching: Did you hear what Peter said? Did you see him show signs of relief? Doesn't that make you suspicious? Your victim shouldn't look so relaxed.

Gloria turns and looks at Peter from head to toe.

Gloria: As I am a professional mugger I have received body language training and am constantly suspicious. I suspect that my victim may be hiding something very valuable in some area of his body.

(She of course gets a huge laugh for this, she's back with her partner and their mutual pretext.)

By sticking to the robber/victim pretext, and with a little more help from me, their game stays on track. Peter and Gloria begin to understand how to develop their own game. By the end of their improvisation they have entered into a partnership,

> stealing something from everyone in the audience. They finally sit on the chair in order to divide up their spoils, which they've accumulated in their pockets, shirts, sleeves, trousers and socks. They have got huge lumps all over them, like Michelin men. The audience applauds them spontaneously, neither has "won" but both are happy.

2. Flow

Improvisation means having nothing prepared, creating as you go along, incorporating the unexpected, using whatever you are given or whatever is on hand. Allowing yourself to flow seems almost too obvious to mention. 'Of course!' you're thinking, 'What else would I do in an improvisation?' But you'd be surprised how often exactly the opposite happens. The human mind is not very flexible until it has been trained. It will, almost immediately, try to fix a set course for you, exhorting you to hold on for dear life to its own precious ideas whilst overruling all signs of imminent disaster. Your mind is actually only trying to protect you from pain, but failing and having problems, making mistakes or acting rashly are the very things your clown needs to do in order to play successfully. Therefore the results of your mind's defence systems onstage are usually disastrous.

For example: You may find yourself making an overtly sexual gesture and before you know it, your mind's morality will have determined that you've gone too far, it'll order you to physically rein yourself in and pretend that the sexy "come on" gesture never happened.

Or you may find that your partner ignores the parameters you have set up for yourself, doesn't understand where you're trying to go or simply does not play along with you; then suddenly you begin to feel uncomfortable and at a loss how to react or act.

Or you may be convinced the audience understands perfectly what you are doing (even though they don't), and continue, come hell or high water, until the teacher eventually stops you with the question, "Is this working?"

All of these are signs that you are still not allowing yourself to flow, not accepting constant change. Somehow you have to convince yourself that *whatever* happens, you'll find the perfect way to deal with it. Having nothing prepared will, without a doubt, give rise to accidents and problems but the audience will love them if you don't block their flow. They will also reward you with their laughter when you do this, be assured. The example I give below shows how an improvisation can work out just as neatly as a prepared sketch if the clowns are skilled in allowing things to flow.

Exercise 5: The super hero/heroine
Two clowns. Before either enters the stage, the teacher places an object on stage. The object can be something either grotesque (a fake bone or hand) or scary (a rubber spider or snake). The first clown enters, establishes contact with the audience and then sees the object. The object immediately inspires their worst nightmare (there's a killer on the loose, they're arachnophobic, etc.). S/he calls out for help.

The second clown is a super hero/heroine (and wears a cloak or pants on the outside, etc.). S/he comes in on the call for help, but instead of resolving the problem s/he makes things worse. The improvisation ends with the first clown saving the super hero/heroine.

Example:

I've left a large rubber fly on stage. Anna comes on, sees the fly and quakes. She starts making a buzzing noise and becomes paranoid; looking around and wildly batting the air with her arms. She loses balance and falls towards the fly. She fakes it's movement, making it land on her arm. Paralysed with horror she cries out for help. Nothing happens. She cries out even louder.

Anna: I need to be saved <u>right now</u>!

The Superheroine, with resignation, steps out on stage. She looks around, deadpan, sees Anna and her problem then sighs loudly.

S: <u>That</u> is your big problem? You called <u>me</u>, to rescue you from a <u>fly</u>?

She turns and walks off stage again.

Anna is totally flabbergasted. She looks at the audience and then at the fly. Her body becomes rigid again.

A: No, please, help me. I'm in danger. Help!

The Superheroine returns but is obviously not keen. She looks at Anna, shaking her head as if she can't believe what she's seeing. She turns to share her disdain with the audience.

S: Lately it's always the same story. People inventing sad little problems and then expecting me to fly in to help them. It's pathetic.

Anna can't believe what she's hearing, she dumps the fly on the floor and strides over to the Superheroine.

A: But it's your <u>job</u> to save me!

She realises that she has no longer got a problem. Hurriedly she goes back to the fly, picks it up and feigns an attack on her jugular. The Superheroine gets more depressed. She walks towards the audience.

S: Actually, to tell you the truth, it's always been like this... even when I was a child. Just imagine how I felt. Terrible. I didn't have a happy childhood... but that's a long story.

She pauses eyeing up the audience.

S: Would you like to hear it?

A: No they wouldn't! They want to see you in action. They want to see you saving me.

She puts the fly down her front then begins to choke and splutter. The Superheroine ignores her.

S: When I was a kid...

Anna falls to the floor and rolls around in agony. The Superheroine turns to look at her and sighs impatiently.

S: You interrupted me. Now I've got to start from the beginning again.

But instead of recommencing her story she recommences the whole of her performance so far. She leaves the stage, and repeats her entrance, gestures, movements and comments until she arrives at the point where she was interrupted.

S: When I was a kid...

Anna has watched it all from the floor. Her anger begins to boil. She pulls the fly out from under her blouse and vents her rage on it. She's turned ninja. She karate chops the fly. It's now on the floor with its legs in the air. She waits to see if it will move again and when it doesn't she becomes victorious, singing to herself the superman theme tune. The Superheroine sighs again.

S: You've interrupted me again.

She leaves the stage again but this time, on entering, she fakes that her cape gets caught on something off stage. She chokes.

S: Help!

The Superheroine plays the moment for all it is worth, exaggerating her difficulties. Anna watches, then suddenly her face lights up.

A: You need help?

S: Yes!

Anna jumps into action, flying around the stage in circles like superman. She sings the theme tune and flips the odd forward roll to try and make the whole thing look authentic. Finally she goes to help the Superheroine, freeing her cloak with a karate chop. She then picks her up in her arms, "flies" once around the stage and heads for the exit. Just before leaving she stops and says to the Superheroine,

A: You know, I didn't have a happy childhood either.

3. Build on what comes up

If you have got a reason for being on stage and are allowing yourself to flow, things will definitely start happening. A game will start, the audience will laugh, your body (often not as protective as your mind) will start playing; it's then that you'll have to begin building the game.

You build the game, bit by bit, through playing the game. How far you can take a given game depends on you, how far are *you* willing to take it? Your clown will be happiest when you go to and past the boundaries and keep exploring. Your audience will be happiest when you fulfil all the promises you make *and* give them even more than they were expecting.

You should aim to keep the game moving, generally forwards, by adding new elements or reusing old elements in new ways. Keep the action on stage, follow your clown's logic (which is not the same as your own), take imaginative leaps, and either incorporate or acknowledge everything that comes up (incorporate what works, acknowledge what doesn't).

Usually it's best to avoid showing the crude reality of things; audiences don't want to see you actually having sex onstage, (though a quick flash of flesh usually gets a laugh), or really picking your nose (though blowing it can be very funny), or really farting (though fake farts are apt to get some people laughing). Apart from that there are really no limits to where you can take a game. It's entirely up to you.

I've used the exercise below with hundreds of students as it really allows them to practise the whole game proposal/ development question. The exercise works for all students no matter what their level, though beginners will need some help in not blocking their own proposals and overcoming creative gridlock.

Exercise 6: Where am I?
As far as I know, Eric de Bont (Holland), was the first clown teacher to use this exercise in Spain.

Two clowns. Two chairs are placed centre stage, and it is explained that they can be used or ignored. The first clown enters, completely at a loss as to why s/he is here, where here is and what s/he is supposed to be doing. If a parallel helps: it's as if s/he has just got out of bed and entered the stage rather than the kitchen. The first clown has thus got to be very present, make a proposal, make contact with the audience, and listen to their reactions. The teacher asks the second clown to enter. This clown also has no preconceived ideas of the where, what or why when s/he enters the stage; the difference being that this time there is someone else there.

Together they have to find the game they're going to play, and build on what comes up. If they can find a good way to end the game and use it to get off stage, they should make the most of it and end their improvisation on a high point.

Example:

Paul enters shivering and takes a slow look about him. He sees the radiator on a side wall of the stage and goes to stand in front of it.

(As it's winter, the audience begins to smile. He has found a game, now he has to build it.)

He hugs the radiator then tries to sit on it but can't. He starts rubbing up against it with his body like a cat.

(The audience is laughing openly now. His individual game is working.)

Sonia enters and looks around, curious. She spots Paul over by the radiator and looks jealous. Then she opens her arms wide in a loving invitation to Paul to try out her wonderful human warmth.

Sonia: Are you cold? Do you need a warming hug?

(The audience likes her proposal. She has accepted his game and added to it.)

Paul thinks over the offer but he's a little wary. He would hate to lose his place by the radiator. For a while he is torn between the appealing hug and the lovely warm radiator. Finally his suspicious nature wins out: he shakes his head at Sonia.

(He hasn't blocked her proposal, merely added a new element that works, the audience enjoyed his exaggerated display of doubt and his internal struggle to come to a decision.)

Sonia, having seen his dilemma and heard the laughter, tries out a very seductive voice.

Sonia: I give amazing hugs. I'm the number one hugger in the country.

She gives herself a hug to prove her point, showing everyone how wonderful her hugs feel.

(She's raised the stakes, and the audience approves. Their laughter means the pair are going in the right direction.)

Paul becomes doubtful again, Sonia's offer is very tempting. It's clear that with a bit more persuasion from Sonia he'll chose the hug. Sonia takes the hint.

Sonia: I'm the World Champion Hugger, 2007 and 2008. Two years running!

Sonia swells with pride and shows him the inside label of her tee-shirt to prove her words.

(Sonia gets a big laugh for the label gag.)

Paul is impressed by her title and moves to receive the desired hug, but she skirts around him at the last minute and agilely skips to the radiator, hugging it on arrival with a squeal of pleasure.

(Paul has accepted the inevitable and allowed Sonia to get the upper hand. The audience laughs their approval.)

Paul staggers about, gutted. After a while his feelings overwhelm him and he slumps in one of the chairs.

(He's played the moment for all it's worth and is enjoying it, the audience is delighted.)

Very slowly he adjusts his body, surprised by how comfortable the chair is. He puts his feet up on the other chair, now totally content. He then looks at Sonia and squeals with pleasure, in an obvious imitation of her.

(The game of "I've got the best place" continues; as it's working there's no reason to change it.)

Sonia looks unsettled. At first she struggles to ignore Paul but her curiosity gets the upper hand. Paul continues exaggerating his physical and vocal expressions of pleasure.

(Now they've reversed roles, a new game within the initial game, and it works, the audience is laughing.)

Sonia, who by now is possessed by the urge to have the chairs for herself, abandons the radiator and moves towards Paul. With a velvety voice she offers him a foot massage. Paul is thrown into a quandary by her feminine wiles, but he forces himself to stay put. Sonia moves closer and strokes his foot.

(She's re-using an old element but with a new slant. It gets a laugh. Now they've got the game structure and a few comic ingredients to play with: role reversal, seduction/betrayal, doubt/pain/pleasure).

Sonia: I'm the World Champion Foot Masseur, 2007 and 2008.

She again shows him the inside label of her tee-shirt. Paul falls for it, lifting his feet and letting Sonia sit. Once in possession of a chair she pushes his feet away cruelly.

Sonia: Ha, ha, ha! You fell for it again. How stupid was that!

(The audience has enjoyed this second status exchange but the clowns need to find a way to end the game. The rule of three applies —any more than three repetitions and it becomes boring.)

Paul is mortally offended by her insult and stands up choking. Sonia takes over the two chairs, a picture of satisfaction.

Paul is furious and begins to stride about. Suddenly he stops dead, his gaze fixed on something off stage.

Whatever it is that he sees, it amazes him. He exits through a side wing and after a pause we hear his grunts of orgasmic pleasure.

(Paul's found the perfect way to end the game without changing it. His proposal is strong but it's up to Sonia to get the last laugh.)

Sonia can't see what it is that's so pleasurable for Paul but she's dying to find out. She jumps up from the chairs and runs to look. What she sees stops her in her tracks, her mouth drops open. We see her jealousy return.

Sonia: Did I tell you I'm also the World Champion Reiki Master, 2007 and 2008?

For the last time she shows her tee-shirt label then exits the stage.

(She finishes the game with a final mix of the ingredients that worked for her, and gets the laugh she's looking for.)

10
Playing together

All the strategies covered in chapter 9 are valid for improvising in duos, trios or larger groups but there are a few other guidelines you'll need to put into practice in order to make game playing with other clowns viable. The first is that you are all in the same boat the moment you get out on stage. The responsibility for making things work is mutual and shared, so you have to think of your partner or partners as team-mates, not as adversaries. All ideas of personal success or outshining the others are simply not helpful here. Throw them out as soon as you can. When clowning, you'll gain many more rewards through cooperation.

'Hang on a minute,' you may be thinking, 'clowns can be very competitive, cruel, and unhelpful. They love winning and can be mortal enemies at times.' It's all true. They can *seem* to be playing on opposite sides; squabbling, fighting, even killing each other, but that's only outward appearances. The truth is that they are secretly working together to attain a mutually desirable goal. They are combining their resources, supporting each other's decisions, and working out a mutual strategy in order to make their audience laugh. That is their goal and they achieve it through the challenge and enjoyment of conscientious teamwork. Stage play in a team is very different from playing on your own but it is not necessarily more difficult. In fact, many students find it easier precisely because they have someone to play with, bounce ideas off, or save them when things get sticky.

Pass the focus

"The focus" is simply where you want the audience to look. If you imagine a spotlight illuminating the action, you'd naturally want to have the spot light on you occasionally. The same goes for your team-mates. Passing the focus means allowing the others a chance to be seen, and it's essential to cooperative game playing. It's also basic stage craft: if you create more than one centre of attention for too long, the audience will overload, you'll lose them and they'll stop laughing.

Chaos on stage, as in too much of everything (sound, movement, words), often occurs in beginners' clown improvisations. But it's easy to remedy. I find if I simply explain to my students that good clown improvisations are very similar to good conversations they normally understand the need to be active listeners as well as able communicators. When improvising you can either:

- have the focus
- be sharing the focus
- be giving or taking the focus

If you have it or are sharing it, you're doing/saying something you want the audience to focus on. The giving or the taking is the moment of passing this focus from one to another. Passing the focus can be as easy as looking at another clown and reducing your vocal and physical output to a minimum, but this is by no means the only way. Below I explain how passing the focus works (in fact all the improvisations in this and the last chapter contain examples of clown "conversations") but the way you do it and when you do it will depend on the game you're playing. It's something to *feel*, certainly not to intellectualise.

Once you've passed the focus on, the audience can still see you so you're never really out of the spotlight if you're on stage. You may not have the focus but you're still on standby. You've got to stay alive and maintain an active interest in the conversation so that you know exactly what is called for when the focus is passed back to you. This will also help you know when you have to jump in and take the focus back (you will see that your team-mate is struggling) or when to do something that shares the focus by supporting the proposal of your team-mate.

Whatever emotion you are playing before you pass the focus feeds on what is being said or done by the others. You accumulate what you're feeling, like a pot on a back burner, so that when you get the focus back again you can simply turn up the heat. Even if your expression is neutral you still absorb whatever's happening onstage so as to be able to comment on it to the audience when the focus is returned to you. Because what you're feeling or thinking is expressed after a pause this can actually be a wonderful way to surprise the audience and get a laugh. Knowing this will help you see that waiting for your turn can be as much fun as having your turn!

Sharing the focus will work, for a short period, as long as your motives for doing so are clear (for example, you are competing, arguing, fighting, being carried away by passion, etc.). Another way of sharing the focus is possible through physical proximity. If you're both playing similar or synchronized emotional or physical rhythms the audience will see you as an entity. Some clown teachers call this working as twins or as a family. Performing like this can be extremely rewarding if the chemistry between you is strong; also, from the audience's point of view, it's truly a delight to watch.

Example of how focus works:
Two clowns. One begins a speech, introducing himself and the show.

He has the focus, the audience watches him.

His partner starts to make fun of him behind his back.

She takes the focus, the audience laugh with her.

The audience's laughter un-nerves the one speaking, he continues his speech but now it is boring and repetitive.

He's giving his partner the focus, reducing his energy and loudness.

She becomes more and more disrespectful in her mockery, the audience's laughter grows.

She keeps the focus.

The other clown begins to feel exposed. Are the audience laughing at what he is saying, or is there something wrong with his appearance, or are they merely laughing at him? He begins to mumble and look confused.

They are now sharing the focus because, although his partner is still enjoying herself she has gone past the high point of her mockery and is therefore losing the audience's interest. Once her energy has fallen a little further the focus returns to the first clown.

The first clown has turned and discovered what is causing the audience's laughter. He throws a look of anger at his partner, maintaining a dominant posture.

He passes the focus back to his partner so that she can react.

His partner shows fear then freezes.

She passes the focus back quickly.

They react to each other in small doses of rising emotion.

The focus passes rapidly back and forth between them.

The situation reaches its climax as the first clown tries to take a swipe at his partner's head. She runs off with the first clown hot on her heels.

They share the focus once again.

Establish a relationship

Whenever two people meet face to face they enter into a relationship. It may be fleeting or lasting, obvious or subtle, fixed or fluid, superficial or profound, but it is always present. If you've ever spent time at a party or at a train station watching people make contact or relate to each other you'll know that you can pick up quite a lot of information about what kind of relationship they have almost right away. Within seconds you can see, for example, how intimate people are with each other. And within the first couple of minutes you'll know what their chemistry is (their levels of mutual attraction or connection), what their individual mental disposition towards the other is (how open, interested, hostile, bored, reserved, etc., they are) and how the others' presence or conversation is affecting their emotional state.

So it would actually look quite unnatural if you didn't show, through your behaviour and emotional attitudes towards your fellow clowns, what kind of relationship existed between you on stage. In fact, in an improvisation, defining your relationship as soon as possible will not only help the audience relate to you, it will help you situate yourselves in relation to each other and therefore within the action, and it will also give you all so much to play with. Human relationships are rich in comedy because they're full of dramatic surprises. If you dive into them on stage, sooner or later you'll be in conflict, or having difficulties and misunderstandings, or you'll find incompatibilities in your mutual needs and desires. In short, you'll start encountering problems, and as we have already seen, problems between clowns can be hilarious.

"Tragedy is comedy, especially when it happens to someone else."

Lila Monti, clown, Argentina

Our relationships with other people are established through a process of individual or joint decisions. When clowning, these decisions can be either:

- given by the exercise itself (you're asked to play specific roles — such as magician/magician's assistant, queen/butler, foreign expert/translator, etc.).
- taken backstage (you decide to hold hands or enter from opposite sides of the stage).
- taken within the first few minutes of your improvisation following your pretext or proposals (for example: someone looks at you with lust or calls you "my little brother").
- allowed to grow within you (you feel out the actual relationship you naturally have with your partner).

When the relationship has not already been given by the exercise, answering the following questions can be helpful in defining your clown relationship:

What is your level of intimacy?
All relationships fall into one of three categories: either they are professional, personal (family, friends, lovers) or are produced through encounters with strangers (someone points a pistol at you or winks at you or tries to sell you something, etc.). Therefore you either know each other intimately or superficially or you don't know each other at all. Any one of these options will get the game between clowns flowing.

What do each of you feel about the other?
Relationships can be either harmonious or discordant. Your mutual chemistry will dictate which of the two it would be more convenient to play. But don't forget that just because you are playing at being husband and wife doesn't mean

you feel positive toward your spouse. Or just because someone is your boss doesn't mean you treat them with respect. You can meet someone for the first time and feel as if you've known them all your life, or you can have lived with someone for years and still not know who they are. Also the way you feel about people can change depending on their actions. Feelings have to be fluid.

Who's playing the dominant role and who the submissive role?
In all human relationships there is an underlying current of energy that can either be dominant or submissive or fluctuating between the two. This is the power you each possess in relation to the other. It can sometimes seem to be non-existent but it is, I can assure you, always present. The balance of power between people has such comic value that I have dedicated the next section to it. For the moment you only have to know it exists and that often the decision you need to take about it is simply the decision to become aware of your power status within the relationship, accept it and play it more obviously.

Clowns love playing out roles; they're like children in this. They'll pretend to be anything as long as it's fun. "Now I'm a... bank robber, juggler, servant, lover, surgeon, movie star." You name it, if the circumstances allow it, they'll pretend to be it. At last, they can be *someone*! So, if you find yourself unable to define your relationship, I assure you, you're resisting a temptation. Remember the inner "yes!" and throw yourself 100% into whatever is being proposed. After all, it is always the clown that we really want to see, the clown having fun. It's like when we watch a child play at being a doctor, we enjoy far more the experience of watching the bizarre imitation being played out in front of us than we do an actual doctor's appointment.

> **Exercise 7: One minute to establish a relationship**
> This is a great, fast-moving game that helps students see how easy it can be to establish a relationship, as long as they are willing to dive into one.
>
> In pairs. Students have one minute to create as many relationships as possible. They start from opposite sides of the stage. At the teacher's signal they run together, create a relationship (doctor/patient, hairdresser/client, bank cashier/bank robber, etc.) then return to their original positions before running in and creating the next relationship. The teacher counts the number of relationships obtained by each pair and the couple with the highest score "wins".

Power or status

Before I explain how to play with status I get my intermediate students to do a simple but fascinating exercise. "We're going to find out who's the most powerful person in the group", I tell them. Immediately there's a shift of energy in the room, people start murmuring, laughing uneasily or becoming fidgety. Power brings up all kinds of stuff in human beings and it's this very "stuff" that makes playing status games so rich and rewardingly funny.

> **Exercise 8: The most powerful of them all**
> One by one I ask them to come on stage and meet the second clown who awaits them there. The clown that is proven to be the less powerful of the two, or to put it another way, the weaker, must leave the stage as soon as s/he realises who's "won". The absolute "winner" is the clown who remains on stage at the end of the game.

I love watching this exercise. I love watching how power manifests itself in individuals, how it abandons them the moment they try to be powerful, how little a powerful person needs to do to assert their power, how power has nothing to do with physical strength or aggressive attitudes, and how obvious it is from the outside who will have to leave the stage.

I usually know exactly who the most powerful person in the group is before they start because they've already demonstrated it, on and off the stage. This certainly doesn't mean that they've bossed people around, or told anyone what to do and how to do it; their power is much more self-contained than that. Powerful people simply own the space around them and own themselves, they are at ease with who they are and have no need to prove themselves to others. They look people in the eye, listen attentively but have their own opinions and are willing to voice them. Some of them are aware of the power they have, others are surprised when they win the game, as if they were born with this ability and think everyone acts as they do.

The exercise is therefore a perfect way of introducing, in a very visual manner, all the basics of power play. Students instantly learn that:

- they have to accept their power in relation to who they're playing with.

- their natural tendency to play high or low status is already present.
- they can have fun no matter what their power level is.
- power levels can fluctuate between people.
- personal power is clearly communicated through body language.
- playing power games on stage can be very funny.

Once these points have been highlighted and discussed, I get the students to act out high and low status clown roles in duos. I ask them to think of roles that automatically create extreme status differences (such as queen and servant, corporate boss and secretary, etc.) so they can really feel the different body language each role requires. Before they begin I also remind them that they are playing together so, as always, they should help each other to have fun and get laughs.

Both the high and low status roles should be enjoyable to play, but those playing the high status role often need to be encouraged to have more fun. The low status characters are the ones who create havoc on stage. They try to do their job well but it's a constant struggle for them, there are just too many opportunities to do everything *but* their job! So they often forget the way they should behave, falling into excesses of enthusiasm, clumsiness, laziness or curiosity. Thus they make everything go wrong for the high status clown, creating problems left right and centre.

The high status roles are authority figures but the audience should love them just the same. Supposedly they are superior in some way, at least this is what they believe — though sooner or later they will demonstrate how ridiculous they really are, usually because of the problems created by the low status clown! The audience is always the highest authority in the room and thus it is the job of the high status clown to maintain his/her dignity in front of them, even when everything is obviously going terribly wrong. They have to express a wide range of emotions in these situations, including self-doubt, anxiety and kindness, to avoid being constantly exasperated.

Exercise 9: Creating problems

Two clowns. One plays a high status role, the other low (duchess and butler, headmaster and pupil, chief and assistant, etc.). The low status clown has to create problems for the high status clown. The high status clown accepts the low status clown's proposals and reacts to them using a variety of emotions. The situation must gradually grow and become more chaotic. Once the game has peaked they must try and find a way to end the improvisation, and leave the stage.

Example 1: The guru and his disciple

The high status clown comes on as a spiritual guru. He exaggerates the stereotype by using a gliding walk and holy gestures. He stops to listen to a voice that only he can hear, conversing with it.

His disciple enters the stage as if in a trance, fingers held in a mudra and humming OM. She does not stop when she reaches the guru but carries on until she arrives at the side wall, here she makes a quarter turn and continues to the back wall where she makes another quarter turn. From here she walks off stage again.

The guru has been watching her with silent incredulity, each time she turns he finds it harder to contain his impatience. When she disappears he takes a deep yogic breath then goes towards the wing curtain to look for her, pretending to be called there by a higher power. The assistant enters from the other side in exactly the same manner as before; when she reaches the guru she turns and walks towards the audience.

The guru is forced to run forwards, losing all his feigned spirituality, to prevent his disciple from falling off the stage. As he holds her by her shoulders, she continues to walk on the spot. He spins her around and makes an exaggerated spiritual gesture in front of her but ends with a violent clicking of fingers in her face.

The disciple awakens from the trance and apologizes profusely.

The guru glides back to centre stage and sits on a cushion in the lotus position. He gestures magnanimously for her to sit beside him. She tries to mimic his position but it's too painful, so she tries other ridiculous postures on the floor, trying to find one that's comfortable. Her final position is flat on her back, using the yoga cushion for a pillow. She immediately falls asleep and starts snoring.

The guru has meanwhile been watching her and losing his composure. By the time she starts snoring he's almost crying. He attempts to pull himself together with another deep breath, then tries to speak above or in between the snores. His disciple drowns him out and changes rhythm so often that he is forced to fall silent. She enters into an erotic dream. Her tongue lolls about outside her mouth, the cushion becomes her lover.

The guru leaps up and repeats the arm movements and finger clicking from before, but this time exaggerating it in length and intensity. His disciple jumps to her feet, her hands once again in a mudra, and begins to walk in her sleep. The OM she hums is interspersed with snores and yawns. She repeats the gag of reaching the walls and turning then exits leaving the guru completely unhinged unable to continue his spiritual charade. He exits in tears.

Example 2: The strongman

The high status clown enters playing a strongman in a fairground. He starts his show revealing and flexing muscles, grunting and growling to highlight the effort involved.

The low status clown, Hugo, enters as an audience member. He is tall with a large build but he's a gentle giant. He observes the strongman, intrigued.

The strongman, pleased as punch with all his bravado, strikes a pose for Hugo, arms in air, showing off his biceps.

Hugo, delicately takes a paper hanky from his pocket and blows his nose loudly. He's about to put it back when he sees it's wet. He tries to dry it by blowing on it but then sees the strongman's arms. He steps up to him and gently hangs the hanky on one of his biceps, meticulously smoothing it out so that it will dry flat.

The strongman pulls it off his arm and throws it on the floor, irritated. He continues with more poses and grunts.

Hugo picks the hanky off the floor and smooths it out. Once again he looks at the strongman and, seeing his brow is beaded with sweat, he carefully presses the hanky there. It sticks to his forehead and covers his face completely.

The strongman reacts with fury this time, ripping the hanky off his face and growling at Hugo. He returns to his show but the intensity of his emotion remains. His grunts have turned into shouts and spittle begins to fly from his mouth.

Hugo is uncomfortable with the level of noise and anger. He becomes tense but even so, seeing the spittle, he takes the hanky from the floor and gently wipes the strongman's mouth. He then tucks it into the top of the strongman's shirt as if it were a bib.

The strongman, as a demonstration of his strength, tears the hanky in half and throws it on the floor again. He makes threatening show-of-strength poses in Hugo's direction. He then yells like Tarzan.

Hugo picks up the hanky pieces, and sticks one in each ear. Obviously, he looks ridiculous.

The strongman senses that Hugo's distracting the audience's attention. He strides over to him and pulls out the bits of paper, snorting his anger in Hugo's face.

Hugo looks at the audience then looks at the strongman. He inhales deeply, assuming his whole height and physical presence, before letting rip a roar. His roar is that of a bear defending its territory.

The strongman looks shocked, then panic stricken. He looks urgently about him, sees the exit sign above a side door, and runs out shrieking like a girl.

Hugo turns to the audience, still bearlike but now smiling. As he leaves the stage he imitates the strongman's poses obviously enjoying himself.

11
The haunted house

If you were to ask me: What's the worst thing about the clown training process? Not knowing if the audience is laughing at you or with you? Failing frequently and publicly? Experiencing the void (those moments when you have absolutely no idea how to proceed)? Revealing parts of yourself you are uncomfortable with? The elusiveness of your clown?

I would reply: No, it's actually none of these things, the worst thing about learning clown craft are the phantoms.

Phantoms?? Yes, phantoms, those spooky apparitions that always seem to pop out at the worst possible moment, for example; just before you're due on stage or when you expect something to be funny but the audience doesn't share your sense of humour. If you've ever tried clowning you'll know what I'm talking about; that motley crew of inner spectres capable of giving you a fright so haunting or unexpected that your heart skips several beats. Furthermore, the suffering they can cause sometimes lasts for far longer than you'd care to admit. To be plain, the worst thing about the clown training process are the psychological ghosts that roam around inside your head; the fears you try to keep hidden (even from yourself).

Lions and ghosts

Fear can be produced in two radically different ways: either by a real threat to your health and well-being, or by your mind sensing a possible threat to them that is not real at all. The physical reactions to both types of fear are exactly the same: accelerated heartbeat, muscle tension, adrenaline rush, dilated pupils, etc. These instinctive fight or flight reactions help us protect and safeguard ourselves in truly dangerous situations, but lamentably, they actually impede our ability to react adequately when our overactive mind makes an unfounded assumption.

If a lion suddenly appears out of nowhere, you need instant help (your senses on red alert, greater muscle strength, more brain power, etc.) because your survival depends on it. If, on the other hand, you hear a strange noise in the middle of the night, the excess of adrenaline and tension will serve only to keep you paralysed in your bed. Your imagination will perceive a ghost where none exists, and you'll remain haunted by the experience until you build up the courage to get out of bed and see that the source of the noise is just a branch moving in the wind.

The brain is a highly sensitive organ that is responsible for sending messages to the whole body through the central nervous system. One of its top priorities is to avoid anything that may cause you either physical or emotional pain. Unfortunately, the brain has a tendency to file the things it finds similar in one, all-purpose folder. Unless otherwise trained, it doesn't distinguish between what's real and what's imaginary, so, if it detects *any* possibility of pain, it immediately sends warning signals throughout the body. If you're the one experiencing these signals first hand, you'll find they happen so fast that you'll only have time to capture the overall message: "Something *terrible* is about to happen!" However, if just at that moment, you step back from the rampant energy trying to drag you into the dark abyss; if you breathe, recapitulate and recognise that it's just a bygone bogeyman rattling his chains at you, you'll find that you can relax and the physical symptoms will fade.

The important role of the heart

Unlike actors, who build their roles from the outside in, creating a life-like representation of a character aligned to the needs of the play, clowns represent themselves. They have to work from the inside out, bringing to the surface all their peculiarities for the audience's inspection. As a result, it's often very difficult for clowns to be objective about their work; it all seems so deeply *personal*. Depending on the individual, it can sometimes take years of clowning experience to gain a clear understanding of what went wrong in a performance and why. The problem could be any one of the following: the material, physical/vocal clarity and skill, the quality of the humour, timing, the creative output, honesty, self-confidence, rhythm, novelty, connection with the audience, or stage presence. For the novice, it can feel as if they are being examined in thirteen different subjects at the same time, and even if they succeed in passing the test on one occasion, there's no guarantee of success the next time round. On top of it all, a clown knows that people will judge their artistic talents on that single performance, as very few will go and see the same show twice. The particular circumstances in which they have to perform (time and place, weather conditions, unexpected technical difficulties, audio interferences, the size and mood of the audience, personal health and mood, etc.) can impact on their ability to give their best performance, but the audience rarely takes this into account. From one performance to another, a clown's overall sense of achievement can vary so greatly that whenever someone says, "I've seen your show", their first reaction will generally be: "Where was that?"

Self-confidence, as I've said, is an important asset when clowning. However, a person with very little stage experience is highly susceptible to moments of doubt and will find the sudden inner tension it can cause quite difficult to handle. Admitting their fear will seem like suicide (after all, they're on stage to make the audience laugh, not to be assured that all is well!), so they'll normally try to continue with the show as if nothing has happened. However, the fear will have shut down their heart and, consequently, their defence system will take over and try to remedy their discomfort. Their performance will alter, either subtly or overtly, in disastrous ways; for example: they will accelerate their timing and all their gags will flop; they will become angry, abusive or rebellious and make their audience tense and unresponsive; they'll become wooden or inauthentic and lose any real connection with themselves and their audience; or they'll hit a blank wall and not know how to continue. The fact that the audience no longer seems to, or actually does not, respond positively to their performance will only further strengthen the fear they're feeling. The audience becomes "the enemy" (the cause of their pain), and from there the whole performance will inevitably enter into a downward spiral.

A clown without an open heart is like a skydiver without a parachute; doomed to a bad end!

Challenging fear

When learning to clown, some of the fears that surface can engulf, overwhelm, demoralize and paralyse even the most robust. Stage fright, fear of being ridiculous, fear of not measuring up, fear of failure, fear of success, fear of being vulnerable, fear of losing control, ugh! No wonder some students initially find themselves thinking: 'Why on earth did I sign up for this course?'

So, what can you do when trepidation tries to possess you? How can you overcome a phantom for good? Entering into battle with yourself (such as attempting to ignore, re-press or crush your fear) is an exhausting option and wastes valuable energy that could be put to better use; such as in loving, listening to and laughing at yourself. I've found that it's more productive to turn towards the fear and take it on creatively. Deep breathing, used in all relaxation techniques, is a strong palliative for the physical symptoms of fear. As for the psychological symptoms, I think there's only one dependable remedy: action. Feel the fear, but get up and go ahead anyway. It really is the quickest way to rid yourself of imaginary dangers. And, the good news is, it will reinforce your sense of security in other areas of your life too. If you move into action, you'll find the "X" on the treasure map. Dig a little and you'll undoubtedly find something valuable to take home with you.

Overcoming fearfulness

In my courses I try to establish an atmosphere of trust and humour that fosters dis-inhibition and honesty. Fear is toxic when confined, noticeably so when clowning, so I encourage students to share what they're feeling as soon as possible. I then help them to express and channel their fear creatively, through their clowns. Naturally, it may take time and courage to loosen deep-rooted fears, so it's important that students listen to their own needs and desires, only moving as fast as they are able. Consequently, while I invite them to accept my help, I respect their wishes; if they feel they're not ready to step into action I do not pressurize them. It is, after all, a known truth that the key to any transformational process is the willingness of the individual to do the work. Choosing to face a fear is of itself a huge first step that deserves collective recognition. Of course, witnessing fellow classmates throw themselves into action and live to tell the tale will also provide the motivation and safety net that hesitant students need to risk doing the same themselves.

What happens when you don't take the ghosts seriously, when instead you bring them out into the light of day, and treat them to a theatrical exorcism? As a clown, you may find yourself reacting to your phantoms in an entirely different way. You'll be tempted to play with them; either representing them as extravagant characters or expressing all the fear you're feeling in their presence. Clowns, given half the chance, will make a meal of a phantom, they'll add salt and pepper and anything else that grabs their fancy; they'll create a whole number around them. Over the years I've seen some hilarious performances by students who have transformed what they were feeling into a work of art. Without a doubt, their fear faded slightly each time they chose to express it on stage and, in the course of time, it disappeared forever.

> "When you play as a clown, you free yourself in a single stroke of all your absurd fears. Once you have exposed your shadow side, what is left? Your luminosity. You become invested with the power of someone who has nothing to lose, because you've already lost it all."
>
> *Alberto Tugores, clown, Spain*

Stage fright

Stage fright is an anxiety, phobia or fear associated with having to perform in front of others. It is produced when someone starts to worry about the possible negative consequences of self exposure in a public situation. The effects of stage fright on the individual are impressive:

- *Physiological:* rapid breathing, abnormal heart rate, profuse sweating, urinary urgency, upset stomach, headache, decreased salivation, dilated pupils, blushing, feeling of closure of the larynx, nausea, general restlessness.
- *Cognitive:* mental congestion, memory failures, self-centred hyper-alertness, exaggerated perceptual judgments, confusion, lapses in concentration, images of failure, rejection and ridicule.
- *Behavioural:* avoidance of action and eye contact, automatic behaviour, slurring or tripping over words, loss of voice volume, frequent or long silences.

Marina's story

Marina was a professional psychologist in her mid-thirties. The first time she walked out on stage she was extremely nervous. Her limbs twitched uncontrollably and she was absolutely incapable of looking at us, even briefly, without her physical discomfort increasing significantly.

She was so completely hostage to her nerves that I felt the best thing I could do was get up and join her. The stress of stage fright decreases when there's someone else sharing the focus of attention. The sense of danger reduces perceptibly and the mind relaxes somewhat. When I reached her, I put a hand on her *hara* (the energy centre located two fingers below the navel), both front and back. Centring the attention in the *hara* activates our vitality and grounds us, so breathing into it is an effective remedy against fear.

I whispered gently: "Close your eyes, plant your feet on the floor, your knees slightly bent. Let your weight drop down to the soles of your feet, feel my hands, forget every-thing else. Breathe deeper and slower. Let your breath expand from your belly down into your limbs. Relax any tension you feel in your muscles." I could feel her heart pumping like crazy while I was talking to her, but that was not the only thing I was aware of; I could also sense the electric charge of positive energy emanating from the group. Instinctively, in absolute silence, her classmates were willing her to overcome her angst; not because they knew her well (it was the first day of the course) but through some natural, instinctive human response; they wanted to see her triumph over her fear.

I kept whispering encouragement in her ear until I felt her pounding heart quieten. I then suggested that she open her eyes and observe the individuals in her audience. "Remember, they may be looking at you, but you're also looking at them. Observe them one by one, slowly. If you feel any discomfort just close your eyes and return to your centre again." Marina opened her eyes and her body remained calm. Breathing deeply, she looked from one person to the next. I could tell that she'd managed to shift her perspective on the situation; she was still the centre of their attention, but her own attention was now centred on herself. She was no longer worrying about what other people thought of her, she was listening to her own needs.

This was an important first step. The more she went out on stage, the more she loosened up. We became the joyful witnesses to her gradual transformation. Any time she felt her nerves taking over, she'd talk sternly to herself, ordering her body to be still. "Who's the boss?" she'd ask her shaky legs. "I am, and I'm telling you to be still!" She had discover-ed, within herself, an unexpected strength, and, judging by appearances, I think wielding it gave her enormous pleasure. Every time she returned to her seat after an improvisation her face was alight; her eyes sparkled and she was smiling from ear to ear.

The root causes of Marina's stage fright were unimportant. What mattered was her determination and desire to make mincemeat of it. She knew she suffered when presenting herself in public and yet she'd signed up for a clown course; that in itself was laudable. Marina, however timid she first appeared, was courageous; she was prepared to turn towards the phantom that had haunted her since childhood and unshackle her bonds. She'd made a decision, turned up and taken action.

Whenever anyone sets a goal and meets it, their self-esteem increases. So, if you are one of the many that suffer from stage fright, take heart! Clowning, a discipline founded in self acceptance, personal empowerment and good humour, is a particularly effective remedy for this particular phantom. Start by setting yourself achievable goals and congratulate yourself regularly. Marina's story is but one of many I could recount; of individuals who were struck down with terror in their first performance but, through perseverance, found release and peace.

Fear of ridicule

Our desire to be normal takes root in early adolescence, when feeling accepted and appreciated within our peer group becomes even more important to us. We strive to look and act like everyone else, hoping to avoid those dreaded labels: freak, geek and nerd. At this stage of our development, we all tend to suffer from pubescent myopia; we rarely look much beyond our own little world. Caught up in a whirl of hormones, we fail to recognise the immense diversity of human culture; that what is normal in one group or nation, may well be frowned upon in another. It is only when we gain a certain maturity that we understand that normality is actually a question of consensus. Supported by a group with which we share the same tastes and interests, we can feel completely normal; even if we are freaks, geeks or nerds!

However, we are sensitive beings, and some of us did not receive enough help or love at the appropriate time. We fell prey to the fear of ridicule, the fear of disapproval for behaving in a certain (outlandish, idiotic, exuberant, spontaneous) way. Sadly, while trying to avoid situations that might make us feel ridiculous, we miss out on the countless opportunities to have fun. Inhibition is the equivalent of self repression; often even natural behaviour gets censored.

Anna's story

Anna came to one of my introductory courses determined to overcome her fear of ridicule. During the whole of the first day she felt self-conscious and awkward whenever she tried to clown, a fact she shared openly with her classmates. She, unsurprisingly, related these sensations to similar ones she'd experienced throughout her childhood. They had left her with a lasting impression that whenever anyone laughed, they were laughing at her, not with her.

After hearing her story, I shared one from my daughter's childhood: "When Amara was little, if she did or said something stupid that made me laugh out loud, she usually had a hard time seeing the joke (and therefore got all pouty about my laughing). At such times I'd say: "Hey thank you so much, you just made me laugh. How fantastic that you can make me feel happy, it's such a great pleasure to laugh!" It took some reinforcing, but she finally absorbed the message; that I was laughing at something she'd done, yes, but that didn't mean that I was judging her negatively or labeling her ridiculous for all eternity. She wasn't a stupid or clumsy person, she'd just done something insignificantly stupid or clumsy enough to make me laugh, and that meant she had done me a service. Once she understood this, she had no problem laughing at herself when something silly happened.

Anna, however, had spent many years reacting with shame whenever anyone laughed at something goofy she had accidentally done. It wasn't easy for her to change the blueprint. On the second day of the workshop I became aware that she was struggling with herself. She forced herself to participate and then labored over whatever task I'd given her, but it was all uphill. By the afternoon I could see that she was exhausted and frustrated, so I took her to one side. "I don't see you enjoying yourself" I said, "and that worries me. Please, don't force yourself to do an exercise if you don't want to. Give yourself permission to sit and relax and only volunteer if you can really go out there without it being a struggle." On hearing my words she began to cry, it was her way of surrendering. As soon as she'd recovered her composure she promised to do what I had asked.

On the third day I saw that her energy had changed, she seemed confident and relaxed. Sometimes these small miracles happen overnight. People, through resting, dreaming, taking a distance or sharing with others, are able to loosen the grip their fear has over them. In her first improvisation of the day she was vital and expressive, able to laugh at her own nervousness. Without the fear clouding her sense of humour, she was hilarious. I could tell she was enjoying herself and enjoying the laughs too. She was also learning a vital lesson. This was how she described her experience in an email she sent me a week later: "And surprisingly, I recognised the clown in me provoking the laughter, enjoying the shame and ridicule, and simply presenting those feelings unabashedly."

It is part of our human nature to want to be loved and seen for who we are, but for that to happen we have to love ourselves enough to show others what we're made of. Anna criticized herself whenever she felt ridiculous, she naturally assumed that others were doing the same. She had associated laughter with cruelty when in fact, laughter is more often than not an expression of love (if you don't believe me, just think about the people close to you who make you laugh).

As far as I'm aware, there isn't a more direct route to healing the fear of ridicule than training to be a clown. Clowns will behave in bizarre and preposterous ways because they don't just want to be part of the crowd; they want to stand out, take up space and other people's time, feel loved. They're naturally generous beings, more so than the norm. Maybe that's why they're immune to feeling ridiculous. If you let your clown out to play, s/he'll see off your phantom; enabling you to give as much as you please *and* receive the love you crave into the bargain!

Fear of not measuring up

"Am I really any good at this?" is a question that people typically ask themselves with regard to their clowning skills — including professionals with years of success under their belts! — and the answer that they come up with will vary, depending on their level of self-esteem. Self-esteem is simply the opinion you have of yourself at any given time. If you have a low opinion of yourself (either temporarily or permanently) you'll undervalue your clowning skills automatically and convince yourself that you're no good or not good enough. You'll tell yourself, even before going out on stage: "I'm going to be terrible. Who am I kidding? I'm not funny. I've no talent". You'll compare yourself with your classmates, with your professional colleagues or with your idols, and will feel even worse: "There are some brilliant clowns in the world, but I'm not one of them. I am mediocre. This is torture, I should give up now".

Please don't dwell on such gloomy fantasies, doing so will just wreck your confidence and your chances of being successful. No-one in their right mind compares themselves to an animal they admire and then berates themselves for not being equally fast, strong or agile. So why do it with your peers? Don't let the dog-eat-dog world out there blind you to the truth. Others may be able to do things that as yet you can't, but your intrinsic value and your unbridled potential are not diminished by this. Your ability to clown is unlimited, except of course by the limits you place on yourself.

Every rung on the career ladder has its pros and cons and the same applies in our profession. Achieving recognition and status as a clown doesn't mean you'll automatically be happier — you may earn more money but because of that people will expect more of you. Also, touring the world may sound wonderful until you've actually experienced it — lived away from your loved ones for months, slept in all kinds of second-rate hotels and eaten what you can, when you can. You might find more happiness and infinitely more satisfaction in performing locally; for your own community, for hospitalized children or for causes that you believe in.

John's story

John was fortunate, in that many of the students in his fellow students were open and confident. This usually helps everybody plunge eagerly into the work, but John held back. He stubbornly acted "the good boy" on stage, which meant his actions and reactions were too insipid to be funny. Obviously, he noticed that what he was doing wasn't working and every now and then, for the briefest of moments, his frustration got the better of him. We smiled at these rare glimpses of his true feelings but all too quickly they were hidden from our view. After only four hours, at the end of the first morning, John was ready to throw in the towel. In the feed-back session he questioned his ability to clown. "Be honest," he said, "will I ever be any good at this?" "Certainly," I replied, "you can become an excellent clown if you stop doubting your capacity to be one."

Needless to say, for some people the road to excellence will be more arduous and take more time than for others. John had accumulated a fair amount of emotional baggage over the years and its weight would slow him down until he released it. The simplest way of feeling differently is through thinking differently, so I continued: "You have to think of it this way, maybe you are not a good clown now, which is hardly surprising after only four hours — after all, this is completely new for you — but the possibility for greatness exists. However, if you place value only on the results you attain right now, you're going to get disheartened. If instead you value the whole process and cease to grade your work in comparison with others, you will free yourself up to simply do the best you can at any given moment. That's going to help immensely."

John smiled when he heard this, and then laughed out loud. When he'd recovered from the great joke he'd just come across, he shared it with us: "I'm thirty-five years old and I have only just seen my own stupidity. How funny is that? I just had a vision of myself at school, hoping against hope to win one of the competitions, to receive a prize that would confirm my worthiness. Can you believe that? I still badly want to win something, to take a trophy home! It's crazy! The next time I improvise, I'm going to be a joyful loser. I think that would be really funny." We all nodded our heads in agreement and encouraged him to try it. The next time he put on his red nose, John let himself play from his heart, enthusiastically revelling in the hopeless, victimized part of himself that was an eternal loser. We, his audience, found his enthusiasm contagious and all his fatalistic comments had us in fits of laughter. He'd turned the table on his phantom and become the victor. He obviously felt he'd taken a trophy home with him that night because he returned the next day, and the next... and now, a couple of years later, he is an excellent professional clown.

Fear of losing control

This is perhaps the most prevalent fear in our society, or at least it seems that way to me after years of teaching clowning skills. I have in fact encountered few people who are completely free of it. We seem to be programmed to want certainty, predictability and solidity even though (or precisely because) we live in a constantly changing universe. In order to establish a sense of security and safety we exert authority over those aspects of our particular world that we can control. Relinquishing control becomes associated with putting ourselves at risk, which is why letting go feels so challenging and sometimes can produce high levels of anxiety.

Fear of losing control can manifests itself in various spheres:

- Control of self: through rigorous standards of conduct, or physical appearance, and guarded emotional expression.
- Control of others: through manipulation, emotional/moral blackmail or aggression.
- Control of one's surroundings: through stocking up, obsessive tidiness, order, planning, or complex security systems.

Clearly, there are forms of control that are necessary for our health and well-being, others that serve to create harmony and order in our society. However, even the powers that be recognise the need for Carnival; a public celebration of chaos and wild abandon. *Carnestoltes* (the character who welcomes Carnival time in Catalonia) is a close relative to the clown; they both love to be reckless, to break the rules, to revel in madness. It's actually an incredibly sane thing to do. It's also fundamental for the creation of any work of art. Inspiration requires holding open a space for possibility. You'll facilitate your clown's ability to be and do all that s/he wants to be and do by not controlling what is possible. If, on the other hand, you place limits on certain aspects of your own craziness, you'll clog up your creative zest and hamper your clown's free expression.

The majority of beginners constrain their clowns by using one or a combination of the following:

- *Intellectualizing*: You think about what to do before doing it: you wait for a good idea rather than follow your impulses, you plan out a strategy before going out on stage, you get blocked when you don't understand what others are doing or saying.

  Antidote: Say "yes!" to everything, be curious, allow for spontaneity, don't prepare anything, do or say the first thing that comes to mind, don't decide in advance what will be interesting to you or your audience, interpret in any way you choose what you don't understand.

- *Blocking:* You block the action instead of flowing with whatever happens: you say "no" to game proposals, you cling to your own ideas, you change the game before giving it a decent chance to work, you don't listen to your partner, you ignore what they suggest, you keep things on safe territory and the scene doesn't progress.

Antidote: Pay attention, try to make something of every game proposal, accept other people's ideas, take risks, allow things to happen, see how far you can take the action, use the formula "yes!... *and...* I can add this!"

- *Imposing:* You tell your team-mates or your audience what to do: you say "do this!" "move there!" "applaud now!", you physically force your partner to do things, you don't allow your partner to participate in the game, you dictate how everything should go.

  Antidote: Be interested in your partner, play on the same team, be caring, suggest and propose, pass the focus, use your creativity to get what you want.

- *Image control:* Your self-image is overly important to you: you always dance in the same fashion, you avoid actions that may make you disheveled or dirty, you hold certain parts of your body rigidly, you steer clear of pulling faces or eccentric movement.

  Antidote: Trust in your capability to survive the mess, be flexible, feel your body's choices, ruffle up or unpin your hair, find inspiration by thinking of someone you know who moves with ease, sweats, gets dirty or wears eccentric clothes *and* is still attractive!

Javier's story

Javier was a thirty two year old Portuguese actor. He was quiet and attentive, with a polished appearance that was always intact. On stage his professionalism was impressive; his movements were clean and precise, his eyes gave expression to the most subtle internal changes and he was always one hundred percent present and interested. He was also a fast learner, assimilating technique and putting it into practice with ease. Consequently, he was able to stay tuned to his clown's frequency and was consistently funny. His clown was an extraordinary combination of child-like innocence and adult lucidity; he stole our hearts with his tenderness and cracked us up with his quick-witted, astute comments.

As the course progressed he became even more adept at using his skills with comic accuracy. When he was on stage, he was like a child in an amusement park; loving every minute of it. He was always the first to volunteer, and seemed reluctant whenever he had to make an exit. Above all, getting into trouble became an evident pleasure, an imp-like grin would play across his lips whenever I berated him for some innocent mischief. In the feed-back circles he was mostly silent, asking only technical questions, but never offering anything more personal. That is, until our very last open discussion, at end of the course; then he shared something that took us all completely by surprise:

> *Today I got out of bed, I looked at the mess of sheets, blankets and pillows, and I decided to leave it as was. I didn't make the bed! That was absolutely unthinkable for me until today. As long as I can remember, I've been unable to see something out of place at home and do nothing about it. I hadn't even questioned it until today. But this morning my clown unexpectedly spoke up, "Leave it just as it is!" At the same time, I suddenly felt a powerful urge to jump on the bed and have a pillow fight with someone. I resisted the temptation, but I think tonight, I'll propose the idea to my roommate!*

Fear of success

Usually we're unaware we have a fear of success; we all want to be super successful, right? Consciously, we may think we want all that success brings, but subconsciously we may actually have some serious reservations about achieving fame and fortune. We may fear:

- losing something: independence, freedom, leisure time, friendships, etc.
- that we will have to change: who we are, our behaviour, our image, etc.
- not being in control: that we will be used, deceived, put upon, etc.
- having to meet other people's expectations: more pressure, stress, responsibility, etc.

Clown students who have a subconscious fear of success will normally reach a certain level and then go no further. They'll constantly sabotage their own development and progress, unless encouraged to face their phantom. People place limits on their own brilliance for one of two reasons: guilt or fear. Guilt is produced when someone thinks his/her success has violated a social boundary or self-imposed limit; for example: "It's rude to openly enjoy yourself when there are others nearby who are suffering", "It wouldn't be right to have more success than my team-mates", "Self-satisfaction is ugly", etc. And they'll feel fearful if they associate receiving recognition or approval with a certain negative consequence; for example: "They won't like me if I'm more successful than they are", "I don't really deserve all this applause and they will soon realise it", "Pride always comes before a fall", "The higher I climb, the more painful it will be when I hit the ground", etc.

If you think you may be suffering from this particular fear, it's useful to get your clown to listen to your thoughts.

S/he will fish out the old beliefs that no longer serve you and dismantle the ones that are detrimental to your progress; s/he'll even give you some good advice on how to be *more* successful! It may seem obvious, but learning how to build on your successes requires you to experience them (along with the failures). My experience, and that of my colleagues here in Spain, is that a clowning career is similar to a game of snakes and ladders. Sometimes you'll be zipping up a ladder, at other times you'll just be plodding along horizontally, and at others you'll be sliding down a snake's back. Guilt and fear have no place in this game. If your conscious aim is to be a winner, then if the dice takes you to a ladder, pray it's a long one!

Berta's story

Berta was a natural, one of those lucky people who are funny in and of themselves. She had an amazing imagination, excellent comic timing and was very articulate. However, she had one major problem with clowning: she couldn't look at her audience. When she sat down after her first improvisation she muttered, "That was pure hell! I felt wretched the whole time." It was strange to hear how she really felt because on stage she'd appeared to be enjoying herself. Inwardly though, the story was playing out very differently; she had felt ensnared in a trap and it seemed that every which way she had turned had only made things worse.

Thinking she just needed some encouragement, I asked the group to give her feed-back: "She was great, right?" When everyone spoke up in agreement, Berta hid her face in her hands, "Nooooo!" she wailed, "aghhhh!!" It was such an absurd reaction that we laughed. At that, she raised her head and peeked at us through her fingers. We laughed again. I wanted to make sure she had heard our laughter, that she knew she had provoked it; "You heard that, right? You heard how appreciative we are whenever you do or say something?" "Yes", she said despondently, "aghhhh!"

On the second day of the course her internal struggle was even more apparent. She hadn't been able to sleep the night before which had weakened her defences; she was thus more acutely aware of her phantom. She still wanted to perform so I encouraged her to look at the audience as much as possible and receive their laughter as a gift of love, but that only made the nightmare worse. Nevertheless, she continued to express all her inner turmoil with such pungent comedy that, even without wanting to, she harvested yet more laughter. We loved her craziness and her honesty, but the more we applauded, the more discomfort she felt. By the end of the day, in her final improvisation, she was unable to even come out from behind the back screen. Even then, she had us in stitches. Having hit rock bottom she finally allowed her clown to express the deep desperation she felt at being valued and all the fear that surfaced every time we applauded. When it became obvious she'd spewed out all of her demons, I sent four strong men from the group to gently lift her up and bring her to centre stage. I then motioned for the whole group to envelop Berta in a hug, and from the epicentre of our circle of love Berta whispered over and over again, "Thank you, thank you, thank you".

Your haunted house

As it's not my intention to mislead you, I won't affirm that you'll be ghost-free the moment you embrace your clown. Phantoms will continue roaming around your subconscious mind, attempting to scare you whenever they get half the chance. They particularly love times of uncertainty and stress, and in our profession there's a whole variety of performing challenges that inevitably create psychological tensions. To mention but a few: how to break the ice/get the ball rolling when your audience is distracted or unenthusiastic; how to maintain your trust when things aren't going well; how to receive open criticism or hostility from audience members with grace or good humour; how to use unforeseen technical glitches to your best advantage. In addition, each new level you reach (your first performance for a paying audience, headlining in an important festival, the premier of a new show, taking part in a television show, etc.) will add a brand new challenge to your list. These are significant career moments, tests of your capabilities and talent, and as such are magnetic to phantoms. It's therefore a shrewd move to take on your phantoms in the early stages of your clown training and learn how to manage the emotions/thoughts/physical sensations they stir in you. Phantoms should not be taken too seriously, nor should they be given more substance than they actually have. If you can recognise them for what they are, wounds from the past that are holding your present happiness to ransom, you can then use that vivid imagination of yours to put a red nose on each and every one of them.

12

Success stories

Although it's true that failure is our clown's constant companion, success is nevertheless the food that feeds us. It's like a chocolate cake filled with cream (or an exotic delicacy, if that's what you prefer) that's just too delicious not to want more of. Once savored, we begin to crave those performances where everything works; when laughter, applause and general appreciation accompany our every move. In truth, it's those oh-so-delectable peaks of success that lure us to continue clowning and working on our skill.

But those who choose to become professionals have to keep the incentive of those successful performances sharply in focus. For most, making a decent living as a clown isn't an easy ride. In fact, it's usually a day to day, month by month challenge that requires a large amount of stamina and resilience. Clowns have to cover their personal and professional needs just like anyone else: they have to eat, invest in their business, pay their taxes, meet their mortgage/rental payments, and buy commodities for themselves and their families. And obviously, covering all these expenses becomes that much easier if they get a job in an important circus, are booked solidly for most of the year, win a prize in an international festival or receive critical acclaim.

Not everyone within the profession, however, has their sights set on this type of world recognition. Many are more interested in using their skills for humanitarian ends or to support social causes. Their struggle to make ends meet is alleviated when the institutions or governing bodies that control the purse strings finally recognise that clowns need to be paid for their efforts. Others in the profession are dedicated to brightening up children's lives or making family events fun. They are helped by a general appreciation of the value of their work and a stable market price that reflects this.

Whatever their specialization, however, I've yet to meet a professional clown whose motives are purely materialist. It's just not possible to be solely interested in attaining money, status, stability, possessions or fame in our business. Clowning is all about the celebration of a free spirit and the triumph of joy, love, foolery and mirth over the accumulation of worldly possessions. Our hearts and minds are thus focused on achieving creative freedom and making a difference in the world; on building community, helping humanity, instigating social and political change, etc. I've asked many renowned professionals what success means to them, and though they've each used different words, they were, in essence, all saying the same thing: "Success is living from and with laughter."

> "Thirty years ago I performed my first show in a public square and have never been able to stop. The dream was of a sun and a sea and a dangerous life, changing the bitter to honey and the grey of the city to colourful encounters with life. I am a happy person!"
>
> *Chacovachi, clown, Argentina*

Exercise 10: The object of your desire

One clown. An everyday object is placed on the stage inside a triangle of white tape. The triangle is larger than the object (about a palm's distance from the object on all sides). It is explained that the tape marks an uncrossable line for the clown and that under no circumstances can s/he exceed the line to retrieve the object. Nonetheless, the aim of the exercise is precisely to gain possession of the object.

The clown is asked to enter the stage, see the object and immediately feel a burning desire to possess it. The desire must be visible, and should grow with every step that s/he takes towards the object. The reason for the craving should be explained, and not just verbally. Why does s/he want that particular object so much? How would s/he use it? How will s/he feel when s/he has it in his/her hands? How is it going to change his/her life?

For this exercise to work, the clown must live the different stages of desire, frustration and fantasy; of wanting to get his/her hands on the object, being thwarted by the taped lines, feeling disheartened, getting excited again by all the amazing things the object will bring, returning to the triangle determined to succeed, failing to come up with a solution, falling prey to despair, trying to suppress the urge to break the rules, feeling the desire within him/her increase in strength, and then finally finding a way to overcome barriers, take the object and revel in the pleasure of its possession before leaving the stage triumphantly.

Human achievement

In clown exercises there are abundant parallels to real life, which is why watching them or participating in them can be so instructive. Exercise 10 evidences the frustrating yet exhilarating cycle of all human achievement; something we often forget when we ourselves are striving to achieve something our hearts are set on. At these times we have a tendency towards tunnel vision. We see someone else reaping success and making it look easy, and want the same for ourselves. We dream that success will come easily, but it rarely does.

The clown in the exercise falls prey to this self-same fantasy. S/he thinks that acquiring the object is all that it takes; that the shoe will enable him to dance like Carlos Acosta, that the water in the bottle will give her superhuman powers, that the hair clip will make her irresistible to the opposite sex. We laugh at the absurdity of such thinking when we're watching the clown, it's so clearly delusional. We know that success in the arts comes at a price, that Acosta may have been born to dance but that he still had to work on it daily, and no doubt had to overcome many difficulties along the way.

In the exercise, the triangle of impassible tape represents the hurdles we all have to face. Although, at first sight the lines do not seem to present much of a difficulty they are, nevertheless, revealed as a huge obstacle that requires all the clown's ingenuity to overcome. But the truth is, we would be severely dissatisfied if the clown simply walked on stage, resolved the problem and made off with the object. Apart from the fact that this would drastically shorten the improvisation, it would also render the achievement meaningless. The same applies to life. It is precisely the challenges we face and overcome that give our achievements real meaning. The obstacles we encounter inspire us to find creative solutions, test our resolve and evolve our capacities. We applaud the clown so enthusiastically at the end because, despite the odds, despite the setbacks and complications, s/he came out on top, triumphant.

The clown's game in this exercise inevitably revolves around what s/he would like to be (a winner), in contrast to what s/he is (a loser). It's a riveting topic because it's so close to all our hearts. Human beings have a built-in defect: we rarely see ourselves as winners for very long. When we achieve something we've worked for we feel elated and energized, but that surge of overflowing happiness soon dissipates. We rapidly get used to our initial state of satisfaction and begin to normalize our achievement. That's why the clown exits the stage in his/her moment of glory. If s/he were to linger for too long, past that initial celebratory moment, s/he would begin to fall back down to earth. Because the next logical action would be to actually try the object out, to see if all that s/he imagined is actually true: can he really dance like Carlos Acosta by putting on that shoe? Will she really drink the water and become a super-heroine? Will the hair clip really transform her into Marilyn Monroe? And obviously, if put to the test, the truth would out, and all the clown's enthusiasm for the object and his/her triumph would drain away.

It is easy to laugh at the cyclical nature of our self-satisfaction with regards to our achievements when we're in a clown class. But we need to learn to keep on laughing when we get home. Our clowns will always find a way of being a winner, they'll always find a simple resolution to the problem in hand. In the case of exercise 10, they might just cover their eyes and sneak their hand over the line (because it's logical to clowns that if they don't see the transgression, the authorities won't see it either!), or they might peel the tape off the floor and push their hand *under* it (the prohibition was "don't cross *over* the line", right?).

What we could therefore take home with us is that we too can find ways to be permanent achievers, no matter how amazing or absurd our achievements are. We can consciously choose to take pleasure in the things we normally overlook: who we have become, the skills we have learnt, the lives we've touched, the fact that we got out of bed this morning, etc. Our dreams of having more or being more are vital sources of inspiration, and without them life would be pretty flat; but the real goal, behind each and every dream, is achieving happiness: something that we can actually give ourselves.

Guaranteed success

If you've scanned the index and come straight here looking for a bottle of pills with an instruction leaflet that states: "For guaranteed success. Take one an hour before putting on a red nose. No side effects", I'm sorry, but I have no pills, not even a placebo. I cannot give you a magic formula for success. No-one can.

I do, however, know that there are certain ingredients, certain human qualities, without which becoming a successful clown would be very difficult. Some of these qualities — such as honesty, presence, imagination, sensitivity, transparency and curiosity — have already been mentioned in different chapters of this book. If you've read it through, you'll already understand that adopting them when performing will make you a better clown. But, on the path to success, there are three other qualities that you will need: resilience: to keep bouncing back even in the face of difficulty; discipline: to train, rehearse and show up on time to gigs; and humility: to learn from your mistakes, other clowns and knowledgeable critics. Your eventual success will also depend on your ability to keep yourself motivated and active, the quantity of funny ideas you can generate, the quality and consistency of their execution, and a true passion for the art of clowning.

> "I could play for an audience for hours. It's what I most love, that encounter, truly connecting, being really in a present that will never be repeated."
>
> *Lila Monti, clown, Argentina*

If you want to dedicate your life to clowning you have to seriously love it; enough to spend hours investigating and refining your art according to the dictates of your own taste and vision. Gradually, you'll have to define the different aspects of your clown's universe: aesthetics, humour, philosophy, physical/verbal language, interests and incentives. If you're starting out it's useful to ask yourself the following questions: What do I want to express? How do I want to express it? What is it that most inspires me when clowning? What do I want to achieve? What are my strengths? Where do I want to perform? What's the age range of the audiences I want to perform for?

My main reasons to clown have been, on the one hand, the freedom it has given me to be crazy and creative; and, on the other hand, the opportunity it has afforded me of investigating the keys to human happiness. From the beginning, I knew it was imperative to take every job that came my way, whether large or small. When the big jobs proved too big for my level of expertise, I did obviously wonder whether I should be doing something else in life. But as soon as I looked around wondering what that could be, I'd always bump up against the question: What other profession could give me so much joy and satisfaction? The answer, as you can imagine, has always been... *none.*

> "Apart from the indescribable pleasure of play-ing, going crazy and transforming oneself into different people and things, the best thing about performing is having an audience that has never seen you before but who may never forget you."
> *Andrés Aguilar, clown, Mexico*

Script it or busk it?

Anthony had worked for several years running in tourist complexes as an entertainer/clown before deciding to attend the clown routine creation course Alex and I gave in Mallorca one summer. Anthony performed six months a year, six nights a week, entertaining multicultural audiences of varying ages. He was, without a doubt, a very talented comedian with an extensive amount of stage experience.

His first improvisation knocked us for six. We were blown away by the explosion of energy and madness that unfolded before our eyes. Everyone in the room fell about laughing with pleasure and amazement, it was evident that what we were witnessing touched on the borders of pure genius. He, however, didn't seem attached to any of his ac-tions. He "threw away" perfectly executed gestures, one after another, changing emotion without any visible seams while maintaining a delightful quality of lightness and play. His tempo was *alegrissimo*, and his performance was peppered with gags. Imagine the following situations one after another at high speed: a majestic entrance, a regal salute to a crowd of thousands, a request for calm, a fit of laughter exploring various rhythms and pitches, a short apology, a gag (pulling out a piece of paper from his pocket, he scrunches it into a ball then says: "origami"), a touch of irony (falsetto laughter at his own gag), a footballer's goal kick to the ball of paper, a 360° pivot, another salute to the multitude, an eccentric walk across the stage and back again, a magician's pose, a magic trick (disappearing his hand in his own teeshirt and making it reappear)...

Throughout this ludicrously absurd train of events he gave the impression that he was absolutely in control, that he was consciously using his expertise to guide his actions. But in actual fact, he wasn't. He was merely surrendering to a moment of pure inspiration. He'd tuned into his clown's frequency and thrown himself head first into the current of adrenaline and endorphins flushing through his body. This had in turn produced a storm of ideas which had swept him up and away. We were a fresh and appreciative audience and our laughter was all the encouragement he needed to keep growing in assurance and craziness.

Having witnessed this one incredible performance, we would never have suspected that Anthony sometimes had serious doubts about his ability to entertain audiences. Privately, he was well aware that his confidence could play hide and seek with him, and that, between performances, a nagging voice inside his head would constantly try to undermine him: "When are you going to get it together? What's going to happen when your inspiration runs dry? What if it happens half way through a performance? What are you going to do then? Remember that time when nobody laughed, how awful that felt?" In other words, he knew he didn't have a safety net, a specific routine or set piece that worked even when he wasn't in a buoyant mood or perform-ing for an audience predisposed to laughter.

I understood perfectly how Anthony felt when he shared his fears with us. For a time I'd performed on the street with only half a show. I had developed a few short routines that worked individually, but as a whole they lacked logic or continuity. To pull in a crowd I'd start with some gags that I knew would attract attention, then I'd present myself and exhibit the one juggling skill I'd picked up at circus school. After that I'd start improvising; stretching out the games I had already found that filled the gaps between one piece of business and another, or making the most of the opportunities that either the audience or a sudden incident gave me. Judging by the crowds I managed to attract, and the money I collected in my hat at the end of most performances, it seemed I had a convincing show; but in my heart I knew it wasn't. I was well aware that my show was insubstantial to say the least, and that its success depended entirely on the degree of inspiration I was able to muster for each performance.

When I was working on the street for myself, when there was no pressure on me to meet anyone else's expectations, my inspiration never failed me. But as time went by, I started getting well-paid gigs at large events, with a responsibility both to the people who'd hired me and the audience who'd come to watch. Suddenly, I became concerned about the possibility of failure; of running out of inspiration with only half a show to save the situation. I knew I was being paid to do a job in which I could play, but my work had to be worthy of payment, it couldn't fall below a certain standard. This demand for consistency made me want to know more clearly what it was I was going to do in my performances; what was going to happen and in what order. I started fantasizing about having a series of predetermined sketches that worked under all circumstances. That's when I decided to create a solid foundation of good material, an exhibition of my talent that would also let me play my favourite game: ad-libbing.

Good ideas

> "A clown needs clear, logical, radical and surprising ideas. The basic work is to really see what happens in an improvisation and find ideas to develop a story — and a surprise to end it."
>
> *Gardi Hutter, clown, Switzerland*

I've seen innumerable clown shows that have failed to entertain the audience due to lack of interesting material. At the most a clown gets an hour to fill, which is not so very long; therefore every minute should count. No-one who goes to see a professional clown show expects to get bored. Audiences hope the clowns will value their time and attention by giving them all that they have got. Personally, the clown shows that have remained with me, months and even years later, were the ones that were full to brimming with inspired occurrences; great ideas done magnificently.

> "All ideas have to be worked on. You make a rough draft of the initial idea, play with that starting point, just to see if you've got something or not, and from there it may begin to become something solid that you can use."
>
> *Toti Toronell, clown, Spain*

A good idea has to be tried and tested: firstly, to see if it's possible to realise; secondly, to measure its comic potential; and thirdly, to make sure the audience will get it. Usually, for every good idea that passes the test and is compatible with the show you're creating, there are dozens of others that have to be discarded or put aside for another time. So, you may be asking, where do all these good ideas come from?

225

"My inspiration is my own universe. My shows
are the result of one question: how can I share
my world view?"

Leandre, clown, Spain

Comic inspiration can strike at any time but most good
ideas result from:
- a solid connection with your clown.
- a thorough knowledge of clown technique.
- taking note of the things you find funny.
- an ability to imagine comic situations.
- observing other clowns in action.
- studying or imitating "the greats".
- your individual talents and strengths.
- doing the things you've always dreamed of doing.
- remembering the child you were.
- improvising around a subject, object, fragrance, piece
  of music or life experience.
- watching comedy shows and films.
- life itself.

Passion

These days, European audiences have cultivated a taste for absolute experiences. Even when they attend a clown show
they want the complete package: fantasy, action, genius,
comedy, poetry, beauty, simplicity and, if possible, mental
stimulation. They want to see a show that flows organically,
with the correct quantity of every essential ingredient, mixed
to perfection, and presented with flair. In short, they want to
see a show created and performed for the love of art.

Your professional success, therefore, rests on your decision
to become an artist; to willingly choose to channel all your
efforts into creating works that reflect the respect, passion

and love you hold for your art. Throughout history, all the greatest clowns have dedicated their lives to refining their performances and their material to the point of perfection. Many started out very young, either born into artistic families or inexplicably drawn to clown. They then spent the rest of their lives perfecting that which most interested or excited them about their art; innocent tenderness, hilarious dialogues, poetic intensity, encountering difficulty, superb gags, comic partnerships or farcical situations. Joseph Grimaldi, Charlie Rivel, Los Colombiaoni, Dimitri, Los Fratellini, George Karl, Grock, Lou Jacobs, Joe Jackson, Peggy Williams, Popov... their names stand for exceptional dedication and quality clowning. Such artists created their own unique style, their own particular image and their own singular material. They have been (and in their wake many others continue to be) true masters of their art, inspiring generations with their vision and version of clowning.

> "It's the norm in any discipline to learn things from someone who knows, and then, over time, make that knowledge truly yours. Reaching that point, where you embody clown technique and perform your own material without copying others, that's what takes time."
>
> *Luis "Loco" Brusca, clown, Argentina/Spain*

A few years ago my husband and I met a Mexican clown company who, after a few drinks, confessed that they'd tried to perform one of our numbers as part of their show. "How did that go?" we asked, already sensing the response we would receive. "Awful!" they replied. "Nothing worked, it was a total disaster!" We laughed, "What exactly happened?" "Oh, it felt completely unnatural, the audience started shouting things and we didn't know how to react. The props broke and flour went everywhere. People started leaving..." As they were actually very good clowns, they continued to expand on the catalogue of disasters and exaggerate their failings. Alex and I found the incremental images of their disastrous experience hilarious but, more importantly, their rehash of the event allowed them to finally perceive their most significant failure; that they had relied on material that was not their own.

It is only natural, when you start out, to steal a gag from another clown or try to imitate the style of a professional you admire, but sooner or later you'll have to tackle the challenge of creating your own routine and finding your own unique style. Although authors such as Tristan Rémy and Pierre Robert Levy, among others, have collected and published many sketches from traditional clowns' repertoires, there are no full length plays written for clowns. This is because clown shows have to be custom made; they have to emerge from the heart, soul, talents and abilities of the person who is performing them.

Without a show that is uniquely yours you will never achieve both public recognition and personal satisfaction. Once it's created, you'll have to be prepared to keep renewing or improving what you have to keep it alive and interesting for you to perform. Your clowning skills will of course evolve naturally over time, but you can fast track this process by choosing to perfect different aspects of your art: the precision and economy of your movements, gestures and words (the practice of "less is more"); your stage presence and charisma; the emotional states and their comic expression; the timing of gags; the dramaturgy; the manipulation of props with skill and ease; the build-ups, set-ups and punchlines; audience stimulation and participation, etc. In the process of mastering all these elements, your passion for clowning will inevitably play an pre-eminent role; it'll propel you forwards, pull you out of the ruts, keep you on track, and help you achieve what your heart is set on.

> "My clown buys me airplane tickets, food and petrol; I owe him my life and my passion for living. Either I clown, or I die."
>
> *Lucho Guzman, clown, Columbia*

Effective clown pedagogy

Obviously, there are many different opinions on the subject of what constitutes good clown pedagogy, though very few have found their way into print. I've drawn my own conclusions from my experience, as a student and a teacher, as well as from talking to other clown teachers over the years, but I'm well aware that it's still a topic open to debate.

My own understanding of the most effective ways to teach clown is constantly deepening. Many of the methods I use and the principles I am guided by are contained in this book. However, apart from the actual structure and content of each class, I have come to believe that there is a third, equally important element. To be an effective facilitator you need to be a living example of the clown fundamentals. For me, that doesn't mean clowning around the whole time so much as embodying the clown spirit: being authentic, admitting mistakes, speaking from the heart, sharing one's own ridiculousness, highlighting the comedy of the moment, being fully present, playing different roles, being mischievous and having fun.

I always take time to prepare my classes but I never let that limit me. I'm well aware that the real teacher isn't me, but the collective of clowns who have gathered to party. If everyone present connects to their clown, I know they'll each

have learnt something useful. To that end, I'm attentive to
when their clown appears and the direction in which s/he
wants to go. My role is to keep encouraging them to open
more doors; to experience and experiment continually. My
aim is to help them remember what they already know
and give them information on how to improve their comic
capacities. But it's a reciprocal act of giving and receiving,
a symbiotic process of mutual discovery. My belief is that
everyone should take away something of value; whether it be
to do with their clown, or themselves, or a specific piece of
clowning technique.

> "I never express myself as if I were a teacher, nor
> do I think I'm giving a class. I'm in charge of
> taking them to find something, but the work is
> theirs. If people want to enter and play, they are
> invited."
> *Gabriella Muñoz, clown, Mexico/U.S.A.*

It is my responsibility to attend to the needs of the
individuals *and* of the group; to see where or why they are
failing individually or collectively, and come up with the
relevant information, exercise or stage experience to help them
overcome the problem. Specifically, I ensure that nobody is
left behind, isolated in their own failure. The people who
need extra help receive it. With their permission, I'll mobilize
the group to support and encourage them, or I'll harness
the talent of the other clowns to imitate, incite, chaperone
or supervise them. The results are beneficial not only for the
individual concerned but for the whole group. Helping each
other establishes trust and *camaraderie,* and the moment of
breakthrough is collectively cathartic. I'll frequently remind
everyone to be patient and not place unreasonable demands

on themselves and I'll encourage them to see the value of the steps they take (however small) *and* of the mistakes they make (however large).

I always want to give students multiple opportunities to put their talent to the test, but the exercises I propose try to take into account the level of expertise I see within the group. If the exercise proves too demanding it will create immediate tension and unease. When I get it right it's also plain to see; people will jump right in, let their clowns loose and surprise even themselves. Because I trust that students come to learn something real, I'll give them my honest feedback after the exercise. I never attempt to whitewash their mistakes or avoid the difficult truths, but I do try to tackle the most urgent of their problems with constructive, rather than destructive, criticism.

Over the years, I've come to understand that students appreciate a brief imitation or recap of the things they did that worked. Beginners often don't even hear the laughter they garner, but even if they do, they rarely know what the audience found so funny. More experienced students may have a better understanding of what was behind their clown's successes, but they still need to have them reinforced and acknowledged.

So, that is usually my starting point, followed by a breakdown of the moments when they lost their clown: when they wasted opportunities to follow up on good ideas or play the games that were working; when they forgot to listen to their partners or pass them the focus; when they failed to share with the audience and played instead a solitary game, etc. I tend to keep my feedbacks direct and concrete. There may be many things to correct, especially with beginners, but to mention everything at once would demoralise them. At first just telling them, "you have to take pauses" or "share your feelings", will be enough of a task for them. I know from my own experience that it is much easier to understand what is being asked of you than to actually implement it! Therefore, I'll usually give them just one or two things to work with but knowing that I may have to repeat the instruction several times before they're able to assimilate it.

Advanced students are more aware of when things went wrong or became uncomfortable on stage, so with them I will usually concentrate my feedback around the question: "How can you improve on what you have done?" Sometimes I'll offer my own suggestions, but I'll also ask them directly if they have any ideas, or open up the question to the rest of the group. This makes for a rich learning environment where everyone can learn from everyone else. In fact, they always do! — because, actually, the best tuition anyone ever receives in a clown class is the live examples performed by classmates; and the real masterclasses, those improvisations that simply cannot be improved upon.

Successful students

The people most likely to find their clowns and let them play successfully in class have one characteristic in common: receptiveness. They're attentive students who genuinely seem to enjoy themselves no matter what they're doing; whether they are performing, observing others perform, listening to commentaries, or offering comments of their own. Their enthusiasm to learn from any source means they have no trouble maintaining their energy throughout the day. They throw themselves into every new activity; unafraid to explore or uncover uncomfortable truths about themselves. They're also naturally sensitive to the needs and feelings of others, and in improvisations, will willingly pass the focus to their classmates and support their proposals. Such students almost always have a well-developed sense of humour and/ or an easy laugh that is generally contagious. Furthermore, each one has a unique gift, a special quality that makes their clown absolutely lovable: an explosive imagination, a range of expressive gesture, incredibly stupid ideas, an enveloping tenderness, a natural wit, a special dazzle in their eyes, etc.

On rare occasions, some of these students have experienced clowning nirvana: they completely surrendered to their clown's foolishness and found themselves immersed in such an un-anticipated level of success that they began "flying". This is the best way I can describe what seems to happen when a person allows their clown to sit in the driver's seat and go wherever they desire. Seemingly, they'll grow wings of pure hilarity and, without exception, whatever they do, say or feel, is side-splitting. In the audience, you're aware that the performer has taken a headlong dive into the spring of their own creativity and has thereby entered into a kind of comic trance, delirious, inebriated on pleasure and laughter. Their sense of humour is so triggered it becomes boundless, inexhaustible, an endless stream of delectable nonsense.

Over the past twenty-five years I've had the privilege of seeing several clowns flying during class, and every single one of them has been etched in my memory forever. Such flights are absolutely amazing to witness. When our ribcages couldn't stand more laughter someone would have to physically remove the clown's red nose because they were unable to return to earth of their own accord. I've wiped years off my physiological clock through laughing at my students' follies, but those who've gone flying have opened a window on timelessness itself.

I myself have had the good fortune to experience this state on several occasions. It is an incredible sensation, like getting into a groove you could dance forever. There's no way you want the music to stop. You sense that the audience adores you, that nothing you can do can fail. Time both stretches and contracts resulting in a feeling of playing in slow motion and fast forward at the same time. You are yourself, but a surprising version of yourself that is skilful, hilarious, focused and absolutely free to express whatever comes to mind. A kind of mystical connection permeates the space and everyone present. And, without anyone having to name it, everyone is aware of its transformative power, of the communal cleansing that is taking place in everyone's energy field.

Experiencing comic enlightenment is not an everyday oc-curence, even for experienced clowns. I love recounting these stories, but they are not the only wonderful success stories in my repertoire. There are many others that are equally precious to me. Clowning leaves no one indifferent. Certainly, the con-scious act of opening our eyes, our senses and our hearts to humour will inevitably change our internal landscape forever. Clowning triggers hidden emotions and encrusted attitudes that have kept us unhappy, but it also gives us the tools we need to return to happiness. The clown awakens a positive force within us that guides us to be less egotistic and more mature in our outlook. So within a very short period of time we begin to notice profound changes in our approach and reaction to life. Many of my students have thanked me after having experienced the life-altering effects of connecting with their own humanity and *joie de vivre*, but it is not me they should be thanking, but the clown: the indomitable optimist, the indestructible altruist, the irrepressible comic master that is within us all.

CPSIA information can be obtained at www.ICGtesting.com
Printed in the USA
LVOW04s1142280915

456015LV00001B/89/P